The Routledge Guide to Working in Criminal Justice

Every year thousands of people compete for employment in the UK. Employability and the ability to demonstrate the skills, attributes and behaviours required in a full-time job have become integral to securing employment and developing a career. This book aims to offer a one-stop guide to becoming employable and to careers in the Criminal Justice sector and beyond, exploring the key organisations and employers in England, Wales, Scotland and Northern Ireland, explaining how they operate and detailing how they are changing.

Written in an engaging and accessible style by four experts on employability and the Criminal Justice sector, this book combines useful hints on becoming employable with helpful insights from those working in specific sectors. The book covers careers in:

- probation
- the Police
- prisons
- the courts, Prosecution Services and advocacy
- youth justice.

Packed with hints and tips, advice from current students, useful web links and lists of recommended reading, this book provides a clear guide to the career decision-making and transition processes and covers the essential elements required to making the first step towards securing a job in the above sectors. It will be essential reading for those who want to forge a successful career in any area of the Criminal Justice sector.

Ester Ragonese is a Senior Lecturer in Criminal Justice in the School of Law at Liverpool John Moores University.

Anne Rees is a Senior Lecturer and Regional Tutor for the Institute of Criminal Justice Studies at the University of Portsmouth.

Jo Ives is Deputy Director of the World of Work Centre at Liverpool John Moores University. She is a Senior Fellow of the Higher Education Academy.

Terry Dray is Director of Graduate Advancement, Employer Engagement and Alumni Relations at Liverpool John Moores University.

'This book offers a new way of thinking about taking up employment in the Criminal Justice sector. In easy-to-follow steps it educates the reader about the Criminal Justice System and provides a constructive approach to decision-making around what type of employment and in which part of the Criminal Justice System the reader may want to work. The authors clearly understand the demands of employment in this sector and engage the reader in a consistently thought-provoking style.'

Dr. Jane Winstone, Principal Lecturer in Community Justice, University of Portsmouth, UK

'This book is a very welcome resource that will be helpful to students, educators, careers professionals and those in the early stages of Criminal Justice careers. It is comprehensive, informative, accessible and very thoroughly researched. The book is organised in a very user-friendly way, with the reflection points, action points and mini case studies being easy to find and helpful to the reader's practical understanding of the routes into criminal justice work.

There are a plethora of useful additional resources, including websites, provided to aid further investigation. A very helpful read.'

Paul Gaunt, Director of Careers and Employability, University of Chester, UK

The Routledge Guide to Working in Criminal Justice

Employability skills and careers in the Criminal Justice sector

Ester Ragonese, Anne Rees,
Jo Ives and Terry Dray

Routledge
Taylor & Francis Group

LONDON AND NEW YORK

First published 2015
by Routledge
2 Park Square, Milton Park, Abingdon, Oxon, OX14 4RN

and by Routledge
711 Third Avenue, New York, NY 10017

Routledge is an imprint of the Taylor & Francis Group, an informa business

© 2015 Ester Ragonese, Anne Rees, Jo Ives and Terry Dray

The right of Ester Ragonese, Anne Rees, Jo Ives and Terry Dray to be identified as authors of this work has been asserted in accordance with sections 77 and 78 of the Copyright, Designs and Patents Act 1988.

British Library Cataloguing in Publication Data
A catalogue record for this book is available from the British Library

Library of Congress Cataloging-in-Publication Data
Ragonese, Ester.
  The Routledge guide to working in criminal justice:
  employability skills and careers in the criminal justice
  sector/Ester Ragonese, Anne Rees, Jo Ives and Terry Dray.
  – First Edition.
    pages cm
  1. Criminal justice, Administration of. 2. Career
  development. I. Title.
  HV7419.R346 2014
  364.023 – dc23
  2014012515

ISBN13: 978-0-415-81070-8 (hbk)
ISBN13: 978-0-415-81071-5 (pbk)
ISBN13: 978-0-203-07075-8 (ebk)

Typeset in Sabon by
Florence Production, Stoodleigh Court, Devon, UK

MIX
Paper from
responsible sources
FSC
www.fsc.org FSC® C013604   Printed and bound by CPI Group (UK) Ltd, Croydon, CR0 4YY

To my dad Dave, my brother Dava and my son Daniel

For Tim, Francesca and Giacomo

For Carol, Oliver and George

Contents

Illustrations

Figures

Table

About the authors

Ester Ragonese is a Senior Lecturer in Criminal Justice in the School of Law at Liverpool John Moores University (LJMU). She spent the early part of her career working in the probation service as a Probation Officer. Prior to her appointment at John Moores, she was a Lecturer in Probation Studies at Liverpool University. Ester has a keen interest in a wide variety of areas but has a particular interest in issues relating to diversity/inequality in the Criminal Justice System, the management and treatment of drug users, the homeless and the practice of punishment. More recently Ester has developed an interest in the issue of employability and within her team takes the lead on this area. She is currently the leader for a module that focuses on Professional Development within Criminal Justice. She has been a speaker at conferences in Britain and in the United States and has been involved in a number of research projects.

Anne Rees is a Senior Lecturer in the Institute of Criminal Justice Studies at the University of Portsmouth. She is highly qualified with a varied career in both the Probation Service and in the field of teaching within Higher Education. During her career in the

Probation Service she held a range of positions including Probation Officer, and acting senior and practice development officer. Anne then moved on to develop the role as lead trainer in the roll out of OASys and Enhanced Community Punishment training to the Merseyside Probation Area. During this period she simultaneously worked part time at the University of Liverpool on the Community Justice BA Hons programme.

Anne has been in her current post for the last nine years, initially involved in the delivery of the distance learning Community Justice BA Hons Programme in the North West region. Following the retendering bid, she is currently part of the Probation team that has developed the new Probation Qualification Framework (PQF) and has responsibility for the North East region. This position has enabled Anne to develop and deliver a wide range of learning and teaching programmes in a variety of styles. She has a diverse range of responsibilities including developing and delivering workshops, lectures, tutorials, marking and attending regional development meetings. She continues to contribute to the development of the PQF and the Community Justice Programme. Her areas of specific interest include dangerousness, drug misuse, women in the CJS and mental health.

Jo Ives is the Deputy Director of the World of Work Careers Centre at Liverpool John Moores University. After teaching for a number of years in secondary schools and Further Education colleges, together with establishing and running a small business, she moved to the newly established Merseyside Training and Enterprise Council (TEC) as the Further and Higher Education Officer for the region. In 1997 she joined LJMU as Principal Lecturer and Manager of the Food Industries Forum, operating an enterprise and training unit within the university.

She joined the newly established WoWCC in 2007, becoming Deputy Director in 2008 and leading specifically with the creation and development of the World of Work and WoW Skills Certificate process and accreditation.

Recently the development work has extended internationally, planning and delivering a successful WoW Skills Certificate project in Malaysia for the Ministry of Higher Education, and with their largest public university, UiTM. She has also undertaken research work with employers in state owned enterprises in Vietnam, in conjunction with Rolls Royce and the British Council.

Over the last three years Ms Ives has written a number of papers related to the work of the centre and WoW Programme developments and has presented at conferences both in the UK and internationally.

Terry Dray is Director of Graduate Advancement, Employer Engagement and Alumni Relations at Liverpool John Moores University. In this role he takes the lead in developing and implementing the World of Work Programme and Alumni Relations. His professional interests focus upon student and graduate employability and career development. He has worked in Higher Education careers services for 20 years and has held management positions at Oxford University – where he was Director of the Career Service, Warwick University and the University of Manchester. He has an MA in Careers Guidance and an MSc in Management. He has served on the Executive Committee of the Association of Graduate Careers Advisory Services and has travelled widely, conducting professional visits and delivering papers in Australia, South Africa, China, Malaysia, Europe and the USA.

Acknowledgements

We would like to thank all the students and practitioners in the field who shared their time, thoughts and experiences. We would also like to thank Steve Burbage, Steve Altham, Louise De La Rosa and Heidi Lee for their support throughout the writing of this book.

Finally a big shout out goes to Wayne Campbell. You're a star.

Abbreviations

BA	Bachelor of Arts Degree
BSc	Bachelor of Science Degree
CJS	Criminal Justice System
CV	Curriculum Vitae
Dip HE	Diploma of Higher Education
FE	Further Education
HE	Higher Education
HESA	Higher Education Statistics Agency
HND	Higher National Diploma
KIS	Key Information Statistics
MAPPA	Multi-Agency Public Protection Arrangements
NHS	National Health Service
NOMS	National Offender Management Service
SIA	Security Industry Authority
SIS	Secret Intelligence Service
UCAS	University Central Admissions Service

chapter 1

Introduction to the book

Chapter objectives

By the end of this chapter you should be able to:

- understand the purpose of the book and who it is written for;
- understand the format and layout of the book;
- understand how to get the most out of the book for your needs as the reader.

By selecting this book you have taken a very positive step to finding out about how to get into a successful career in Criminal Justice.

This book has been especially written to help students like you in both Higher and Further Education, who may be journeying through education for the first time, or returners to education wanting to change your career direction. The aim is the same, to help you find your own personal route into a fulfilling career in Criminal Justice. Many of you may already know the type of jobs that you want to do, some of you may still be considering what your options are and we hope this book will also help those who have yet to make up their minds and are looking for rewarding and fulfilling graduate employment but have not yet decided where this may be found.

Gaining graduate employment in any sector can seem quite a daunting prospect today, the once tried and tested routes via college, university or direct training programmes have become more varied and far less certain than 10 or 20 years ago.

Reflection point

Think about these definitions:

A widely accepted definition of employability is a set of achievements – skills, understandings and personal attributes – that make graduates more likely to gain employment and be successful in their chosen occupations, which benefits themselves, the workforce, the community and the economy.

(ESECT – Enhancing Student Employability Coordination Team, based on Yorke 2006)

Employability is not just about getting a job. Conversely, just because a student is on a vocational course does not mean that somehow employability is automatic. Employability is more than about developing attributes, techniques or experience just to enable a student to get a job, or to progress within a current career. It is about learning and the emphasis is less on 'employ' and more on 'ability'. In essence, the emphasis is on developing critical, reflective abilities, with a view to empowering and enhancing the learner.

(Harvey 2003)

The type of graduate work on offer and the expectations of employers are not always obvious to new graduates, and this is coupled with what appear to be complicated recruitment and selection processes used by many large employers in both the public and private sector to sift through the growing numbers of applicants, which often adds to the fog. It is hardly surprising many graduates consider finding a graduate job similar to finding your way through a maze, with many false starts and barriers that seem to prevent you from reaching your ultimate goal – a graduate job.

This prospect should not deter you from seeking the career you want in Criminal Justice. Yes, the world of work is changing in many ways, in every sector and Criminal Justice is no different in this respect and this is likely to continue. It is one of those facts of life that can often make it seem confusing at first glance but the thing to remember is that you can succeed; the roles on offer are many and varied, providing both challenging and fulfilling careers.

You have taken the first step to finding all the information you may need to make your choices and this book will give you some ideas, suggestions and tips on where else you may want to seek further information. Additionally plenty of careers advice and guidance is also available, from both formal and informal sources, at colleges, universities and online, as well as by talking to staff and individuals who work in the sector.

Action point

Take the time to seek out these opportunities and use the information to make a clear plan for yourself and ensure you are as well informed as you can be to navigate the route you want to take.

This book has been written to try to de-mystify some of the information to help you make your choices and to provide some practical guidance that you may need to find your route to graduate employment. It will provide you with some clear hints and tips on how to overcome some of the barriers you may find in your way and how to get ahead of some of the competition by making sure you understand what employers are looking for, and how you can best demonstrate you meet these demands.

It may help at this point to be clear about what we mean when we talk about the Criminal Justice sector as a potential employer, as it's a very broad and encompassing title. So to be clear from the start, this book will look at the key agencies and organisations that are fundamental in the UK Criminal Justice System, covering over 400,000 jobs. These core agencies are the Police, the Crown Prosecution Service, the Courts, the National Offender Management Service (including both prisons and probation services) and the Youth Justice Board. Additionally some services are run and managed by a number of voluntary groups e.g. Victim Support and National Association for the Resettlement of Offenders (NACRO). These agencies collectively work together to provide Criminal Justice, i.e. where crimes and criminals are detected, detained, tried and punished, at both a national and local level.

At a government level, the work of these agencies is the joint responsibly of three departments, and these set out and oversee our national policy. The Ministry of Justice oversees the magistrates' courts, the Crown Court, the Appeal Courts, the Legal Services Commission and the National Offender Management Service, which is responsible for both prisons and probation services. The Home Office has the responsibility for the Police, and the Attorney General's Office oversees The Crown Prosecution Service, the Serious Fraud Office and the Revenue and Customs Prosecutions Office. This book will detail how the Criminal Justice sector in the UK is organised and managed in much more detail and some of the key issues likely to impact on its operation in the future, which may have some fundamental changes to the way the sector is run and what jobs and roles will be open for graduates in the future.

If you are serious about a career in Criminal Justice, then having a clear and comprehensive understanding of how the sector operates, who are the main employers and what types of jobs are available are some of the key pieces of information that will give you a significant advantage, and ensure you seek out the jobs that best suit your particular interests, skills and ambitions. First, selecting an appropriate course of further study, if you have not already done this, but also seeking suitable work experience opportunities to develop your skills and add to a greater understanding and knowledge of the sector, will assist

introduction to the book

your recruitment, application and selection process. This book has been specially written to help you in all these areas giving you a clear introduction and insight to the sector, the employers and what they want and expect from new graduates.

The book has been researched, written and compiled by four professionals who bring many years of practical, personal and academic experience from the Criminal Justice, Higher Education and Careers sectors. Together these individuals have brought unique insight into the changing world of Criminal Justice and linked this with the sector specific and more generic employability skills required by graduate employers today and highlighted the tools and techniques needed for you to transition successfully into the sector.

You will find detailed information on key employers and organisations operating in the sector, their vision and mission as well as their size and scale. The book will outline clearly the range of roles and careers available in them as well as the skills, knowledge and competencies that will be required to successfully undertake these jobs. It will give you up to date information on how to apply and what the recruitment process will involve as well.

The book is intended to be a very realistic guide on what is happening in relation to jobs and employment in the sector and how you can access these opportunities. It will offer you practical advice from individuals who know the sector well and who work closely with employers to identify the changing needs of the sector and how employers are looking to recruit to meet their demands. It will also give you some idea of what these jobs are like on a day-to-day basis and what you would be expected to do in a typical day's work, highlighting what skills and personal attributes are likely to be needed to work in these roles and undertake the challenging responsibilities.

You will also find some case studies from students currently studying Criminal Justice and related studies, who give their personal views and reflections on what to consider when you are thinking about what course to study and how to choose the course that suits you best and, perhaps most importantly, hints on how to optimise your studies and make the most of your time while on your programme of study.

Your inside knowledge and information about the Criminal Justice organisations, employers and the nature of the jobs is only part of your career planning picture; to be successful you will also need to understand yourself and why you want to work in this sector, for these organisations and with these clients. It's worth remembering here that getting a job is a two way process, it may well be about demonstrating your knowledge, skills and abilities to successfully undertake the role but it is also about how you will 'fit in' within an organisation and its culture.

> ### Reflection point
>
> Working in Criminal Justice can be a very rewarding personal and professional career, but it will also bring many challenges and have you really thought about this aspect? What is your motivation for wanting to work in this area, can you explain this? What do you think you can achieve in this type of work and is this realistic? If these are questions that you currently cannot answer, then you will find this book can help you think and reflect on your career path.

You may be thinking these are questions that you don't need to answer yet if you are just starting on your career planning, and you won't need to articulate the answers until you fill in an application form or go to an interview. You will need to be able to do this later in your journey but you do need to seriously think about these now and this book can help as these are fundamental to your career goals and direction. If you are unsure about why you want to work in this area or with these agencies, other than it sounds like a good career option or you have seen the work on TV, then take some more time to think about this. It may well be a good career choice for you, hopefully this book will make you think about what attracts you to the type of work and why. You may not have sufficient information to answer these questions now but this book aims to guide you through these issues and prompt you to think clearly about yourself, your skills and abilities and your ambitions and to ensure you have sufficient information to make the right choices for a successful career in Criminal Justice.

> *ichelle, 2nd year student, Criminal Justice*, 'Be very clear about what your aim is in life. Understand what the course is about and where do you want to go? CJ is an ambiguous title and is a very big field of work; it's very complex and some people appear to have a very fixed idea of what it is. Try and understand this complexity before committing to a degree.'

> *arah, 2nd year student, Criminal Justice*, 'It is a tough area to work in so make sure you prepare for this work and the client group, as it can affect you mentally. You need to be open minded and not judgemental, as this may not be the career for you.'

This book is aimed at you, in thinking about where you currently are in your career in Criminal Justice and where you want to be, as well as how you get there? Hopefully it will inform you, challenge you as well as giving practical help and guidance to get you closer to where you want to be – a successful career in Criminal Justice.

However, you may find once you have read this book you decide a career in Criminal Justice is not for you, which is a positive outcome, as the book is not only designed to give information and guidance about the sector, the jobs available, and how to access these. It is also designed to challenge your thinking and motivations about why you want to work in this sector, how much you know about the type of work and, as part of any good career planning guide, its task is to ask questions about your self-awareness, personal and work values as well as your motivations. Don't be tempted to leave this section out, as it's crucial to your future plans and career. Many people embark on courses and sometimes jobs without fully understanding what they involve and whether they are well suited to this type of work and personal commitment. You may be fixed on finding a career or a specific job in this sector, it may look and sound very appealing, but digging a little deeper into your motivations for wanting to work in this sector is a very worthwhile exercise, at this stage, and will help you in the future to formulate applications and to respond to interviews.

The Criminal Justice sector is very broad and encompassing, so it does have a wide variety of jobs and career options and you may not have decided upon one route or career, which at this stage is understandable. This refining of your options and career paths will probably start to formulate when you are studying, it will also be shaped by the work experience opportunities you take and the volunteering or placements you become involved in: all of these opportunities are aimed at developing your skills and knowledge as well as identifying jobs and roles you enjoy and those you don't.

The sector is very competitive and it may be that your first choice of career or role is difficult to access initially, even with a good degree, so you may need to consider other options and possible routes of entry for the longer term. This is the same for many careers and the key is to understand the personal skills, knowledge and aptitudes that you have developed and bring to a role, and if necessary find alternative opportunities and jobs to gain more experience.

How to use this book

You can start here and read your way through all the chapters or you may just want to pick out certain chapters relating to organisations that interest you most. In the book you will find highlighted text and text in boxes to aid your reading and to pick out key themes, as well as tasks or things to note.

You will find *reflection points*, where you may need to stop and think, as well as *action points* that flag both *activities* you can undertake and *actions* to help you progress. Most chapters have some *'top tips'* if you want to quickly look at these in addition to comments from students, graduates and practitioners working in the Criminal Justice sector, to help you get a better understanding from those already studying or working in the area.

Don't forget to look at the employability sections as well, which show how to make yourself employable. The route into a job will require you to have knowledge, skills and competencies as well as a good understanding of the organisation and the jobs you want to apply for; after all, employers employ an individual and not just the degree or subject discipline. They expect that person to demonstrate a range of skills and competencies within the job role and they actively seek these when they are recruiting, so make sure you know what these are and how to demonstrate them.

Finally, good luck in developing your career in the Criminal Justice sector, we hope you find it both challenging and rewarding.

Top tips

- Use the boxes to navigate your way around the text and to help you understand some of the key issues being discussed.
- A reflection point box gives you an opportunity to stop and think.
- An action point box gives you an exercise or task to complete.
- A speech bubble is information directly from students or practitioners aimed at helping you to understand some issues or at sharing their experiences.
- Top tips are at the end of each chapter to highlight the key points that have been made.
- Useful websites and recommended reading will be included at the end of most chapters.
- Refer to the list of abbreviations at the front of the book, which is a useful summary of key words used in this field.

References

Harvey, L. (2003) Transitions from Higher Education to Work: A briefing paper prepared by Lee Harvey (Centre for Research and Evaluation, Sheffield Hallam University), with advice from ESECT and LTSN Generic Centre Colleagues

Yorke, M. (2006) *Employability in Higher Education. What it is – and what it is not.* Learning and Employability Series One. York: ESECT and HEA

chapter 2

Introduction to the Criminal Justice System

Chapter objectives

By the end of this chapter you should be able to:

- understand the concept of Criminal Justice;
- understand how the agencies involved in the Criminal Justice System work together;
- identify the principles that underpin the Criminal Justice Process.

Introduction

In this chapter we intend to introduce you to the concept of Criminal Justice. It is an issue for all of us and developing an understanding of the processes, systems, structures and agencies is crucial if you intend to work in this sector. In its most basic of terms the Criminal Justice System works together from the commission of an offence to the point at which someone has served their sentence. Involved in this system are a number of different agencies and processes that operate at different points.

What is crime?

Crime is:

'An act or omission constituting an offence (usually a grave one) against an individual or the state and punishable by law'

(Oxford English Dictionary 2014)

It would appear at first glance that crime can, and is, easily definable. Therefore we could presume that there would be no criminal activity as society should be aware that if they commit an offence they will be punished. Why then do crimes occur? And why are some crimes defined as such?

Although the definition above of crime does not specifically state what action or omission constitutes an offence, surely it is common sense that we know right from wrong and which crimes should be punished. It is most certainly naïve to suggest that this is true, so too is it incorrect to think that all individuals will abide by the law because most individuals in society have different interpretations as to what constitutes a crime. What this demonstrates is that crime is in fact very difficult to define, because not only do people have differing views but the concept of what a crime is changes over time and between societies. It has only been since the late twentieth century that legislation was passed to amend existing laws and thereby decriminalise homosexuality. Even so, despite it no longer being a criminal offence to be homosexual, there are members of society who oppose this. Again this demonstrates how difficult it can be to define crime, when what constitutes a crime and evidentially what does not provokes continual disagreement between individuals across society.

Who commits crime?

The reason(s) as to why someone may commit a criminal act are not only complex but plentiful. There is no single cause for all types of criminality – there are a plethora of factors as to why an individual may become delinquent. Although by no means exhaustive, the following are some of the more common underlying causes of why an individual may commit crime:

- influenced by drugs and/or alcohol
- to provide for one's family
- for fun and excitement
- influenced by peer pressure
- lack of legitimate opportunities
- to fund a drug dependency
- due to discriminatory beliefs
- learnt behaviour from parents, family, friends and/or sources of media
- to seek revenge following being previously victimised.

Just as there is no one single cause as to why someone commits a criminal act, there is no one type of individual who commits crime. For instance, it is wrong to assume that only males can be paedophiles and likewise it is wrong to believe males cannot be victims of domestic abuse. What these examples highlight is how crime can be caused by any individual within society, regardless of their age, gender, social class and/or appearance. This hereby exemplifies how those who commit crime are not a homogenous group.

Reflection point

Write down what you believe are the typical traits of an offender. In your opinion why do think crime is more likely to be caused by an individual with these characteristics?

What principles underpin Criminal Justice?

The Criminal Justice System is based on two key principles; the adversarial principle and the principle of due process. When thinking about how the system operates it is important to consider both of these principles.

The adversarial principle

The adversarial principle is based on evidence and the way that evidence is used in deciding which cases go to court and what happens when in court. Listed below are some of the key factors that determine how guilt should be established:

- accuser/accused
- sufficient evidence
- beyond reasonable doubt
- burden of proof
- standard of proof.

Reflection point

The adversarial justice concept of beyond reasonable doubt not only ensures the innocent are protected against any wrongful conviction, but also protects those who are guilty in instances where the evidence cannot be found and is therefore not available to prosecute the accused. Think about how this makes you feel, and whether you agree that the Criminal Justice System in the United Kingdom should be based upon proof and not truth.

Due process

Due process is based on a person being innocent until they have been proven to be guilty in a court. Listed below are some of the key principles that underpin due process:

- fairness
- innocence until proven guilty
- formal and open adjudication
- values
- justice.

How does the Criminal Justice System operate?

The following figure is a depiction of the Criminal Justice Process within England and Wales that immediately proceeds from a crime being reported to the Police. Essentially, this is a suspect's

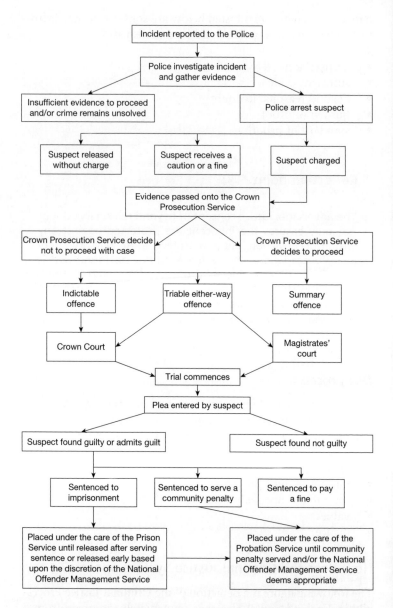

Figure 2.1 The Criminal Justice Process in England and Wales

journey from their initial contact with the law, inclusive of the ways in which the agencies of the Criminal Justice System are involved at each of the various stages within this process and how they do or should work together.

Although the previous figure was a concise overview of the Criminal Justice Process within England and Wales, there are in fact three considerably distinctive Criminal Justice Systems within the United Kingdom, those being Scotland, Northern Ireland and England and Wales. Even though each of these Criminal Justice Systems operates with different laws and procedures, as well as differing agencies (although they do undertake similar functions), some overarching policy and functions are definitive as they are implemented at a national level duly coordinated by The Home Office.

At a local level, The Home Office places responsibility for overseeing Criminal Justice within the three jurisdictions of the United Kingdom to the following Ministries; The Ministry of Justice (for England and Wales), The Justice Department (for Scotland) and The Department of Justice (for Northern Ireland). In order to provide clarity upon how the agencies within these jurisdictions of the United Kingdom compare and contrast, each of the main agencies of the Criminal Justice System (those most central and visible agencies) will now be discussed in turn, and they are: the Police Service, the Courts and Prosecution Service, the Probation Service and the Prison Service.

What agencies are involved in the Criminal Justice System?

The Police Service: In England and Wales the powers that the Police Service have at their disposal in order to conduct their role both effectively as well as ethically is outlined within PACE, The Police and Criminal Evidence Act (1984). In Northern Ireland, Police Officers operate under highly similar codes of practice as outlined by The Police and Criminal Evidence Order (1989). However, in Scotland there is fundamentally no legislation that is comparable to PACE. In respect to who oversees the Police Officers, each regional Police force within England and Wales as well as in Northern Ireland is overseen and led by a Chief

Constable. However, additionally in England and Wales, it is also the duty of a locally and publically appointed Police and Crime Commissioner to then hold Chief Constables to account for their force's performance. In Scotland, the legal responsibility for overseeing policing within each regional Police force is not solely that of an appointed Chief Constable, but also that of Scottish Ministers.

The Courts and Prosecution Service: Each of the three Criminal Justice Systems within the United Kingdom is wholly adversarial in nature. Under an adversarial justice framework, it is the role of the Prosecution Service to prove beyond reasonable doubt that the accused is guilty. In England and Wales the Crown Prosecution Service is the state agency entrusted with this undertaking, they were formed in 1985 by way of The Prosecution of Offenders Act. Whereas in Northern Ireland the Public Prosecution Service who were established in 2005 carry out a similar role, as too do the Crown Office and Procurator Fiscal Service within Scotland. Those whom these Prosecution Services need to convince is all dependant upon the court within which the trial takes place. In England and Wales, as well as Northern Ireland, if this is a magistrates' court then this will be a group of lay magistrate judges, alternatively if the trial is within a Crown Court then the decision lies with a jury. However, the court system in Scotland differs somewhat, as rather than magistrates' courts, Scotland has courts known as Justice of the Peace Courts. Similarly to a lay magistrate, a Justice of the Peace is not legally qualified and must therefore be assisted in their decision-making by a legally qualified Clerk. Likewise, instead of Crown Courts, Scotland has courts called Sheriff courts whereby responsibility rests with a Sheriff and a jury to take into account the evidence presented to them in their deliberations. Unlike in the courts throughout the rest of the United Kingdom, the accused in Scotland has no choice in whether they are tried by a jury or a lone Sheriff.

The Probation Service: Probation services throughout the United Kingdom are those deemed accountable for providing adequate supervision for those offenders serving community sentences, as well as overseeing those offenders recently released from custody. In 2008, the probation and Prison Services in England and Wales were consolidated to form a new agency – the National Offender Management Service. In Northern Ireland probation services are orchestrated by a separate body entirely – the Probation Board for Northern Ireland, which was established in 1982 by way of The Probation Order. It not only comprises probation staff, but also representatives from the local community to oversee the operations and legitimacy of the service. While in Scotland, Probation Officers are labelled Criminal Justice social workers and despite the difference in name they fulfil a highly similar role as Probation Officers within the United Kingdom.

The Prison Service: Parallel to the other Criminal Justice agencies that have been discussed in detail thus far, there are also separate Prison Services in England and Wales, as well as Northern Ireland and Scotland. Nevertheless, despite this being evident, throughout all jurisdictions in the United Kingdom the core underlying principles and functions of prisons are considerably alike. In addition, regrettably all jurisdictions share the same problems too, such as fundamentally having to adapt and respond to a rising prison population, while attempting with enforce a productive and humane regime despite a severe imbalance between the quantities of staff in comparison with the sheer amount of offenders. Ultimately, irrespective of the jurisdiction, it is strongly considered that fundamental change is deemed imperative within the Prison Service.

Reflection point

For more information and clarity about the above agencies including their roles, responsibilities and figures please refer to the relevant chapters in this book.

Action point

Considering that the United Kingdom has three distinctive Criminal Justice Systems, including three separate Ministries for the separate jurisdictions, do you believe that it would be considerably more effective and efficient if the entire United Kingdom used a universal system, overseen by a single Ministry, which was a combination of all three existing systems? What would you say are the positives and negatives of doing so, and why?

What are the models of criminal justice?

In order to address and understand the differences between what the law states should happen, 'the law in books' and the way in which the Criminal Justice System operates in practice, 'the law in action', a series of different theoretical models of Criminal Justice, have been introduced. These models provide a general overview and therefore do not necessarily reflect what happens in practice but emphasise how most Criminal Justice processes can be influenced by them. The models are also an expression of the values held by the various Criminal Justice Agencies.

In no particular order the models of Criminal Justice are:

- *Due process model (justice)* – this model represents an idealised version of how the Criminal Justice System should work as derived from the rhetoric of the law. Under a due process model, the primary function of the Criminal Justice Process is as arbitrator of conflicts between individual and State.
- *Crime control model (punishment)* – the primary aim of this model is to prevent the occurrence of crime through the use of punishment. The precise degree of punishment inflicted under a crime control model is one which takes into account the extent and magnitude of the harm caused by the accused.

- *Medical Model* (*rehabilitation*) – under the medical model, the consideration is establishing the greatest means possible to reduce the criminality of an offender. For it is considered redundant to punish offenders without identifying and attempting to address the reasons for the offender's criminality.
- *Bureaucratic model* (*management of crime*) – the focus of the Criminal Justice System under this model is one of placing finances to the forefront. This model states that it is acceptable to flout some rules of law in order to solve crimes, process offenders and ultimately please the public that justice is being delivered.
- *Status passage model* (*denunciation*) – this model claims that an offender's trial and punishment should be made public in order to degrade and facilitate the loss of status for the offender in the eyes of those members of society who are law-abiding. This will in turn reaffirm the moral values of society and enhance solidarity and lawfulness.
- *Power model* (*maintenance of class dominance*) – according to the power model, the Criminal Justice System is a tool by the ruling dominant classes to promote and reinforce their interests and beliefs, culminating in their unyielding dominance over the rest of society. In doing so, the Criminal Justice System, both its laws and the enforcement of these laws, are used to protect the dominant classes from the working class who constitute the majority of offenders.
- *Justice model* (*just deserts*) – linking both crime and punishment to issues of morality and control, this model focusses upon the importance of punishing offenders based on the seriousness of the offence committed, as opposed to merely imprisonment, as it is the ultimate sanction that may not be justified depending upon the actions of the offender.
- *Management model* (*offender control*) – combining rehabilitative practices with surveillance and control, the management model focusses upon changing an offender's behaviour while not forgetting that some offenders are not susceptible to change and should be monitored regardless of whether they are remorseful for their previous actions.

Which one of the above eight theoretical models do you think is the best representation of the Criminal Justice System, and why?

Which one of the above eight theoretical models do you think the Criminal Justice System should portray, and why?

Chapter summary

In reading this chapter you have been given an overview of the Criminal Justice System that will now hopefully inspire you to read the succeeding chapters of this book. This introductory chapter began by discussing the difficulties that exist with defining crime, then led onto explaining the principles that underpin Criminal Justice within the United Kingdom: adversarial justice and due process. This was followed by a brief outline of some common reasons as to why an individual may commit crime, as well as the ways in which crime is recorded and measured. The chapter then explained the three distinctive Criminal Justice Systems of the United Kingdom, including some of the agencies involved, and how they compare and contrast dependent upon the jurisdiction. The chapter then concluded by making reference to the eight different theoretical models of Criminal Justice that seek to justify how the Criminal Justice System can operate.

Top tips

- Thoroughly research the sector of Criminal Justice that you are interested in.
- Think about the way in which the Criminal Justice System operates.
- Understand the difference between the Home Office and the Ministry of Justice.
- Think about the principles that underpin Criminal Justice practice.
- Think about whether the Criminal Justice System is in fact a system or a process.

Some useful websites

- www.gov.uk (The Home Office and The Ministry of Justice)
- www.crimesurvey.co.uk (The Crime Survey for England and Wales)
- www.scotland.gov.uk (The Justice Department, The Scottish Crime and Justice Survey, and Criminal Justice social work Services)
- www.dojni.gov.uk/index (The Department of Justice, the Northern Ireland Crime Victims Survey, and the Northern Ireland Prison Service)
- www.police.uk/forces (The Police Services of England, Wales, Scotland and Northern Ireland)
- www.justice.gov.uk/about/hmcts (HM Courts and Tribunals Service of England and Wales)
- www.scotcourts.gov.uk (The Scottish Court System)
- www.courtsni.gov.uk/en-GB/pages/default.aspx (Northern Ireland Court and Tribunals Service)
- www.cps.gov.uk (The Crown Prosecution Service)
- www.ppsni.gov.uk (The Public Prosecution Service)
- www.crownoffice.gov.uk (The Crown Office and Procurator Fiscal Service)
- www.justice.gov.uk/about/noms (The National Offender Management Service)
- www.pbni.org.uk/site/Home.aspx?x=eTyoYPm5488 (The Probation Board for Northern Ireland)

Recommended reading

There are a wide range of resources that cover the Criminal Justice System. We have chosen these texts as they are accessible, easy to read and easy to understand.

Cavadino, M., Dignan, J. and Mair, G. (2013) *The Penal System. An introduction.* 5th edition. London: Sage

Ellis, T. and Savage, S. (2012) *Debates in Criminal Justice: Key themes and issues.* Oxon: Routledge

Gibson, B. and Cavadigno, P. (2008) *The Criminal Justice System. An introduction.* 3rd edition. Hampshire: Waterside Press

Joyce, P. (2013) *Criminal Justice. An introduction.* 2nd edition. Oxon: Routledge

Maguire, M., Morgan, R. and Reiner, R. (Eds) (2012) *Oxford Handbook of Criminology.* 5th edition. Oxford: Oxford University Press

Marsh, I. (2011) *Crime and Criminal Justice.* Oxon: Routledge

Newburn, T. (2013) *Criminology.* 2nd edition. Oxon: Routledge

Whahidin, A. and Carr, N. (2013) *Understanding Criminal Justice: A critical introduction.* Oxon: Routledge

Reference

Oxford English Dictionary (2014) 'Crime'. Oxford: Oxford University Press

chapter 3

Routes into Criminal Justice careers

Chapter objectives

By the end of this chapter you should be able to:

- understand the range of academic routes into Criminal Justice;
- find detailed information on the courses available;
- identify sources of student funding for these courses;
- identify the right course options for you;
- learn how to make the most of your chosen course of study;
- identify some of the apprenticeship opportunities in the sector as alternative routes to a career in Criminal Justice.

Like many students reading this book, you may be planning for your career journey to include going to university to prepare you for working in the Criminal Justice sector in the UK, and for the majority this will be the case, but there are other opportunities and other routes that are available, and it's worth considering them alongside the more traditional routes to make sure you have chosen the right route for you.

At this stage of your studies you may think all programmes and courses offered in Criminal Justice at different colleges and universities are the same or very similar, but this is not always the case, so researching the options available is essential and also about the places you can choose to study as well.

If you are a student in England contemplating going into Higher Education you will be expected to pay tuition fees for your course, if you are a student from Scotland, Wales or Northern Ireland you need to check out the student fee arrangements for your country, and those that relate to you. Most students now take out a student loan to cover these fees, and we will not cover the funding of this area of HE programmes in this book.

Action point

If you want to apply for a student loan you will need to check out the appropriate agency depending upon where you live.

www.slc.co.uk is the website for The Student Loan Company for the UK

www.saas.gov.uk is the Student Award Agency for Scotland

www.studentfinancewales.co.uk is for Student Finance Wales

www.studentfinanceni.co.uk is for Student Finance for Northern Ireland

The majority of fees are £9,000 per year for university undergraduate programmes in the UK. Over an average three year programme this will add up to a minimum of £27,000, many students may also take out additional loans for maintenance or to cover living/accommodation costs, as well as some personal overdraft facilities. All of this is now part of the accepted HE landscape in the UK, however it is worth mentioning that this amount of money is equivalent to any major lifetime purchase you will ever make and is a significant personal commitment for you in the long term. Therefore do check it out before you embark on any course of study and make sure you have considered all the options available and what are the likely outcomes from the course. You wouldn't go and book a holiday or buy a new car without some significant research and consideration of all the options you have available. Students today are looking for value for money so make sure you know what this means for you.

Reflection point

Think about what value for money this will represent for you. What do you expect to get for your money?

This chapter will outline what things you need to check out. First, it would be useful to think about *the nature of the course you want to study and also where you want to study*, this may be local or involve a move to a new city but also consider the type of Higher Education institution as well. Some universities for example are on a single campus, with all teaching/lecture rooms as well as your halls of residence and accommodation, sports facilities, bars and shops also on the campus – these are usually located a few miles outside a city or town. Other universities are city-centre based with no specific campus perimeter, with buildings for teaching located in different areas across a city, all universities have their own 'feel' about them and character, some are very modern and some more traditional so you will need to factor in what suits you, and this may not be what suits your friends so try to check out any choices for yourself before making any final decisions.

You will need to think about the course and qualification itself. Within the UK in 2013 there are over *40 different Higher Education providers offering degrees or higher level qualifications in Criminal Justice, and related topics*, these range from both

Batchelor of Arts (BA) and Batchelor of Science (BSc) degrees to Higher National Diplomas (HNDs), Diploma of Higher Education (DipHEs) and Foundation degrees. The choice is both wide and varied, most of the degree programmes are offered over three years of study, with one or two offering a 'sandwich' year or year out where you undertake paid work related to your studies – this is a placement or internship. Some universities find these opportunities for you, in others you are encouraged to find and apply for these independently. The HNDs and the DipHEs are usually offered over two years of study.

> *A*my, 3rd year student, Criminal Justice, 'I looked at other university courses in Bangor and Edge Hill and Cumbria, and Criminology courses as well as other programmes and I only decided on my current course when I had visited the open day, visited the city and spoken to staff about the programme.'

> *N*atasha, mature student, Forensic Psychology and Criminal Justice, 'Do your research and look at the university's prospectus and league table information. Go and visit the city as you will spend a lot of time there. Find something that feels "right" for you, go with your instincts.'

> *D*ave, mature student, Forensic Psychology and Criminal Justice, 'Too many people pick a city they want to live in and not the course itself. You need to understand what you want to study and then look at where you can study it. Think carefully about where will the degree go, and lead you?'

It's worth remembering that Higher Education providers are not always universities, as some are colleges that offer both Further Education programmes for 16–19 year olds mostly, as well as some Higher Education programmes. These Higher Education programmes are often validated and offered in conjunction with a local university but are delivered on the college campus, by suitably qualified college staff. The programme is overseen and accredited by the university and while providing the same content, may offer a different delivery programme/schedule from the same course offered at the university. The fees may also vary to those charged by the university, they are usually less, as students do get the same course content but will not be able to access the full university student experience as they would do if they studied full time at the university campus e.g. careers information, advice and guidance may be provided by the college and not the university; this may mean students do not have access to more specialist graduate advice and guidance or this may be limited. This study option may be worth considering as it has many advantages, it may be more convenient for you if you don't want to move away from home or have other family and personal commitments and travelling locally suits you better, or if you prefer a smaller college setting for study rather than a university, as well as saving on the cost of your studies. Some of these two year programmes may also offer a 'top up' year at the university that would give you the opportunity to complete a full Batchelor degree at a later stage. The nature of the programmes on offer to students also needs careful consideration, in the main the degrees are offered as a single subject, Criminal Justice. However, many universities/colleges offer joint and triple subjects. This may give you the opportunity to consider a specialism within your programme of study.

Action point

Use the UCAS website www.ucas.com to find the current list of Criminal Justice related programmes on offer.

Programmes of study can include Criminal Justice with one or more of the following:

- Applied Social Science
- Crime
- Criminology
- Forensic Criminology
- Forensic Psychology
- International Relations
- Law
- Offender Management
- Police Studies/Policing
- Politics
- Professional Investigative Practices
- Psychology and Social Justice
- Sociology
- Social Policy
- Youth Justice.

It is worth taking some time to think whether you want to study a single subject or if you want to link your studies to a particular career area (e.g. Police Studies or Offender Management), if you want to broaden your studies to include Psychology, Sociology or Law etc., if you have enjoyed studying these previously and want to continue, or whether they may provide more scope for career prospects when you leave your studies.

*S*arah, 3rd year student, Law and Criminal Justice, 'I have always been interested in CJ but wanted also to learn the basics of Law. I feel this will broaden my career options with a joint degree. Make sure you know what you want to do: if Law is your main orientation, then don't do a joint degree, do a Law degree. A joint degree is very demanding, with two different ways of teaching/learning needed. Law has a more formal structure and CJ is more relaxed with theories and research, even the referencing systems are different, Law is Oxford and CJ uses Harvard.'

*R*ebecca, final year student, Law and Criminal Justice, 'Although many universities offer a joint honours of Law with another course similar to Criminal Justice, check if it is a qualifying Law degree because if it's not and you would like to be a solicitor the GDL (conversion course) can be very expensive.'

*S*tevie Louise, final year student, Forensic Psychology and Criminal Justice, 'I chose this course, as I was undecided between Law and Psychology. It seemed a specialist area and linked my interests in Law and Psychology. It was my first choice and I applied for Psychology and Criminal Justice courses as straight subjects as backup. One of the best things about the course is the diverse modules, you are studying a Law case one day and cognitive neuroscience the following day.'

Remember, a combined programme may give you some flexibility and future potential, however the two areas of study may be quite different and may be taught by different staff from different disciplines who teach in different ways, so this is something you may want to ask about as part of your research into the programme and whether you would find this mix of study modes motivating or challenging.

Start to look in more detail and study the programme(s) you are interested in, you should find this information on the individual university or college website.

Action point

Check out each university website and their course finder links where you will get more information.

Take time and look carefully at the *modules or units of learning* and see if the programme and content is what you would expect. If you are not familiar with some of the vocabulary, it is worth doing more in depth research to familiarise yourself with the terminology, this will help you as you contrast and compare the various courses you are interested in. Also look at all the levels of study and what you will study each year, not just the first year, as you will be able to see if you have any opportunities to choose optional modules as the course progresses to align your studies to certain career choices, and if a sandwich year is included, or if shorter placements and work-based learning are included and supported within the programme.

*T*ammy, new graduate of Criminal Justice, 'Find something to study you really like doing and are interested in.'

*S*tevie Louise, 3rd year student, Forensic Psychology and Criminal Justice, 'Dedicate time investigating the course content and the modules of study as well as the different years of study, compare and contrast these on other courses and see what suits you best. Also the options in the future, career wise, look deeper into course and career options as you might need to include extra specialist areas for certain career choices.'

Placements or work-based learning is very important. Employers of new graduates will be seeking those with qualifications and experience, so it is a factor you should consider. Research shows that the most employable students from any discipline are those who have a year placement or internship. This opportunity gives you the chance to put theory into practice and is just what employers are looking for when you apply for jobs, not just what degree you have but what related work experience you have. Criminal Justice employers are no different, in fact the nature of the work in this sector means it's vital to get as much varied work experience as you can. You may prefer to choose a course that has this element built into it, rather than looking for other voluntary work placements outside the curriculum during your course.

Check out the UCAS website and the specific university websites as well and find out as much as you can about the course and content and whenever possible go to the university/college *open days* to ask questions that you may not be able to answer using the online information.

Action point

Find out about the university open days you are interested in well in advance. If you can't make the day, most universities will let you make a visit at another time. However, an open day is especially designed to give you all the information you need as a prospective student.

The students we spoke to when compiling this book found this to be one of the most useful ways of selecting their courses, by visiting the campus and speaking to the staff and other students.

Open days are offered for a reason, they are tried and tested and it will give you an opportunity to look at the institution, its buildings, living accommodation, resources for work and play and speak to the staff. This element can be critical in confirming your choices, what may look good on paper or online may not live up to expectations when you get there and talk to the staff and students. Conversely what may not have been top of your shortlist, ticks all the boxes and everything you have been looking for, it's friendly, the staff are approachable and they can explain what the course is about and what the opportunities are like when you are looking for job, as well as how the institution will help you with your studies and your career aspirations. Remember you are paying fees for all these things, so think about your value for money and what you are looking for.

*L*eah, final year student, Criminal Justice, 'Go to the open days and meet the staff who will be teaching you, look into the course content and the modules you will be studying and how you will be studying. This will give you a much better idea of the course than looking at a prospectus or website: not all courses are the same.'

*M*ichelle, 2nd year student, Criminal Justice, 'Go to the open days, look at course content and look at other courses to help filter out the options. Speak to staff, go prepared to ask questions and speak to people.'

*A*my, 3rd year student, Criminal Justice, 'Use the UCAS website and search the system, take your time and if you find a city or course you like the look of, then visit for the open day and check it out. It can be overwhelming if you are not prepared for the course. Use the open days to get additional information and meet other prospective students, so when I joined the course I recognised a few familiar faces and it made the transition easier.'

*S*arah, 3rd year student, Law and Criminal Justice, 'On visiting the open day I met staff who were "passionate" about their subject and CJ and this is what sold me this course.'

If you get a shortlist of programmes you are interested in, you can then use the *UCAS key information set data* provided to compare and contrast the courses at various institutions. This is invaluable data and is based on the previous leavers from that specific course. It shows employment and career destinations/prospects, degree qualifications and much more and is provided by the Higher Education Statistics Agency (HESA) to UCAS, and is not directly from the university, so can be seen as an objective view of the course from the student perspective.

Action point

You can access this information via www.unistats.direct.gov. uk/find-out-more/key-information-set or look at the key information set (KIS) data for each course on the university website.

All the university *course profiles via UCAS will list the entry requirements* for the individual courses, so make sure you look at these as well, as they will differ, you may need to factor in this information in preparing your shortlist.

Remember *the two year programmes for HNDs and DipHEs may not have the same entry requirements as a Batchelor degree*, so this may be an alternative starting point if your entry qualifications may not meet the University entry requirements at this stage.

If you are a mature student, over 21 when you are planning a career in Criminal Justice, then it may be worth talking to one of the course team at the college or university you are considering about mature entrants. In some cases, if you don't have any recent equivalent qualifications for entry, the recommended route into a Criminal Justice degree may be via a *one year Access to Higher Education course at a local Further Education college* – these are specially designed for mature students who have no recent study history and prepare students for the nature and rigours of study in Higher Education. If they complete the

Access course successfully, for many students these programmes also give them a guaranteed offer of a place at a local university on agreed courses. Students don't have to take up these offers and can look elsewhere via the UCAS system but for many this is an ideal and ready-made supported route to Higher Education, which is locally based, so may suit your needs.

> *M*ichelle, 2nd year student, Criminal Justice, 'I didn't want to study Criminology and didn't want to move away from home to study as I am a mature student with other commitments, so I took an Access course at a local Community College, which included English and Maths.'

> *T*ammy, just graduated in Criminal Justice, 'As a mature entry student I took an Access course at a local FE College – including Law, Psychology and IT studies. As I live locally I applied to go to my local university so this was my first choice. However, once in university it was very different from the Access course, and I feel the Access course "spoon fed" students and it was quite different in HE.'

In some cases you may be offered a place without completing an Access course, depending upon your individual qualifications and circumstances, so you would need to speak to the programme staff to see if this is possible. For many mature entrants, even with equivalent qualifications, they find it very helpful to spend a year on an Access course to get back up to speed with full time study and it also identifies if they will be able to commit to three years of full time study.

Again, if you are a mature student you may want part time study rather than full time and not all programmes will be offered in a part time mode, so it is something you would need to check. Some programmes may be specially designed to be offered as a part time programme of study. However, other full time programmes may be studied part time. As a part time student you would select a limited number of modules each semester and you join the full time programme, you would probably take five to six years to complete an undergraduate degree that is usually three years full time. This can work well if you are highly flexible with your other commitments outside the programme, as you may need to change your study days from semester to semester as your module selections change.

Foundation degrees are also worth checking out, as they may provide the entry level to the degree course you are interested in and you may not at this stage of your studies have the entry requirements for an undergraduate programme.

Don't forget *scholarships and bursaries*, as many universities and colleges offer these grants to students who are studying with them: what is on offer and how much will vary from institution to institution as these are not national awards. Unlike student loans these grants are not repayable so they are 'free' money, aimed at supporting students in their studies and can be used towards your tuition and living costs. Many HE providers will have information on how and when to apply and what grants or bursaries they have, many will be targeted towards specific students: mature, care leavers, disabled etc. and some scholarships are for recognising outstanding student achievements, in both academic or extra curricula fields – they are worth checking out as they may be applicable to you.

Action point

Check out the range of bursaries and scholarships that each university or college offers, they will differ so don't assume they will all offer the same. You may find you are eligible for a grant. Don't assume they will give you the funds automatically; often students have to apply and meet the criteria for the award. This money is not repayable.

Apprenticeships

If going to college or university at this stage is not for you, then you may want to consider an *apprenticeship in this sector*. *Apprenticeships offer a job with training*, so if your career aspirations at this stage are to get some experience and find out what working in the sector is like for you, then this may be a way forward, before you decide to go on to higher level studies.

In 2013/14, according to the National Apprenticeship Service, there are more than 250 types of apprenticeships that are suitable for over 1,400 different job roles, and many are in the Criminal Justice and related areas.

Action point

Check out the website to get a full and up to date list.
www.apprenticeships.org.uk

Look for health, public services and the care sector, types of apprenticeships on offer and the NVQ Frameworks from level 2 to levels 4 and 5 (higher level learning). Look at the following sections for suitable opportunities in your area:

- children and young people's workforce
- Courts tribunal and prosecution administration
- custodial care
- legal services
- policing
- witness care
- youth work
- volunteer management.

The apprenticeships advertised will be updated regularly so it is worth checking a few times to see what is on offer. These opportunities will be recruited too, in a similar way to jobs, unlike a course at a college or university, so you may need to complete an application form and go for an interview and there is likely to be competition for the vacancies on offer.

This is where you may be asked about your reasons for wanting to take a job with training in this sector, your future aspirations as well as your motivations for this type of work. If there are only a limited number of apprenticeships on offer, to beat the competition you will need to provide clear evidence that you have the right aptitude for the work.

This route may be a good way to start your career if you are uncertain about committing to a degree at this stage or you want to gain some first hand work experience in the sector before going to university. The pool of apprenticeships is growing annually across many sectors and it's expected to become a more formalised route for many 18 year olds leaving school and college. However, many apprenticeships are open to more mature entrants so don't be put off this route if you are over 18.

Direct entry into jobs in the Criminal Justice sector

Within the individual agency chapters later in this guidebook you will find details of the jobs and roles that are available via direct recruitment into the individual organisations. Details are also given of the entry requirements and the recruitment processes for each agency.

Chapter summary

This chapter started with an explanation of the academic routes into a career in Criminal Justice. The text outlined all the key considerations for students wanting to pursue these routes and how to find out all the information you will need to choose the best course of study for you. It highlighted the options of where to study and the types of institutions that offer Criminal Justice and related courses as well as the variety and range of courses that are available, from foundation degrees to part time study. It also covered how to find out more detailed information on these different routes from these institutions and how to compare these courses to help you in your decision-making. Non-standard entry routes to these programmes are discussed for mature students. Practical information is included about making the most of university and college open days to get the most out of your research and help with your final choices. Apprenticeships or jobs with training as alternative routes into Criminal Justice are also included, and how to find what opportunities are available to you and how to apply.

Finally direct recruitment and entry to organisations within the Criminal Justice sector are briefly touched upon, but the specific details regarding these are found in each of the individual chapters later in the book. The chapter is illustrated with comments from current students, sharing their experiences, from planning and selecting a course of study to how to make the most of your studies.

Top tips

- Keep up the pressure and don't 'switch off' in between years of study, try to keep focussed.

- Try to get a balance and have some fun, manage your time wisely, get support from friends and tutors and use the help they offer.

- University prepares you for the future and your career path therefore if you want success at the end of the line you need to work for it. Finally take up every opportunity that is offered to you as in the long run it will pay off and you will reap the reward when you go for that interview and you have more experience than the next candidate.

- Mix work and play, you are paying for this course and experience so make the most of it but go to lectures, as it is easy to get behind in studies – get out of bed!

- Enjoy the experience as you won't get this chance again, so work hard and make friends and take all types of opportunities for volunteering and try to 'shine' at university – make the most of it.

- Use your initiative, and all the information that is provided, like programme and module handbooks; the information you need is all there. Use the library and the offers of support you are made or ask if you need help – the tutors will help.

- It is a very demanding course with little time to enjoy 'being a student' as you need to be very focussed. If you can get a volunteering opportunity even in a local youth club this can help.

- Find work placements as soon as possible as these are valuable for thinking about areas you may want to go into. Also complete these before you begin university and in the first and second year so you can allow your final year to be entirely focussed on your studies.

- Read around the subject to understand it better. Use the facilities; go on the extra courses that are on offer as extra curricula activities.

- Treat your studies like a job – 35hrs a week, don't leave work and stick to deadlines. Attend your lectures. You never know more than your lecturers at whatever age you are.

- Ask for help with anything you do not understand as that is what people are there for, but also use your own initiative and problem-solving skills as in the workplace this is what employers will expect.

Some useful websites

- www.saas.gov.uk (Student Award Agency for Scotland)
- www.studentfinancewales.co.uk (Student Finance for Wales)
- www.studentfinanceni.co.uk (Student Finance for Northern Ireland)
- www.slc.co.uk (Student Loan Company for England)
- www.ucas.com (University Central Admissions Service)
- www.unistats.direct.gov.uk (Higher Education Statistics Agency)
- www.apprenticeships.org.uk (National Apprenticeships)

Recommended reading

Kingston, B. and Chalton, N. (2009) *The Complete University Guide: Student finance* (In association with UCAS). Right Way

UCAS (2012) *The UCAS Guide to Getting into University and College: Everything you need to know about the entire research and application process.* 2nd edition. Cheltenham: UCAS

Reference

NAS-P-10005 (2014) National Apprenticeships Service. www.apprenticeships.org.uk (accessed 27 May 2014)

Becoming employable

Finding and securing a challenging and rewarding job in the Criminal Justice sector that makes the most of your attributes, skills, competencies and experiences will demand that you are highly organised, well informed and tactically aware, and you know how to manage the process of successfully applying for a job. Where do you begin?

Making a career decision

Career decision-making is a life-long process and can be influenced by many things at different stages in life, like the condition of the economy and the state of your chosen occupational sector, whether you have the necessary requirements sought by an employer, your ability and willingness to be geographically mobile, your social and domestic commitments, aspirations, your ability and willingness to embrace new technologies etc. The DOTS model of career planning developed by Bill Law and Tony Watts (1977) of the National Institute for Careers Education and Counselling is a well-known and well-used approach that shows how career decisions can be managed. It serves as a good example of career development learning and has four stages, which are:

D: Decision-making and planning – decision-making styles, influences, responsibilities, consequences, goal setting
O: Opportunity awareness – occupations, industry, labour market, education and training
T: Transition learning/implementing plans – job search, applications, CVs, interviews, networking
S: Self-awareness – interests, values, skills, personality and abilities

DOTS, as an easy-to-remember acronym, is useful but to use the model for career planning meaningfully and in a more logical order you would need to take the stages out of turn to reflect on your level of self-awareness, i.e. your personality, strengths, weaknesses, values, skills, capabilities, interests, preferences, values and motivations – those things that make you who you are.

Reflection point

Reflecting on your emotional intelligence is also important:

- How do I interact with others?
- How aware am I of the feelings and reactions of others?
- Do I appreciate the impact of my behaviour on others?
- Do I modify my behaviour around others?
- Who am I?

Once you have a good understanding of who you are and the things that are important to you then you need to know how to access information about the opportunities available, including the state of the labour market and the economy, industrial sectors and occupations.

Understanding the sector

What's out there?

When you have researched and considered these opportunities you need to use your self-awareness to identify opportunities that are achievable and might best suit you. Decision-making skills are required to formulate your list of preferred opportunities and you will use different information and preferences to inform this e.g. influences, responsibilities, consequences, type and size of organisation, purpose of the organisation, opportunities for training and development, salary, the organisation's values etc. If opportunities in your chosen field are limited, this is when you may want to think about a temporary compromise, perhaps considering a job below your planned target level but relevant and useful for your longer-term career development. You may also need to think about the benefits of volunteering. Volunteer roles can bring great benefits, particularly if they are in an occupational area that is highly competitive and that demands previous relevant experience – so this is decision time! The final stage is to make the transition from where you are into one of your preferred roles and organisations. This requires you to have knowledge of how to optimise networks, successfully manage selection and recruitment processes and have a toolkit of effective methods such as how to write the best type of CV, letters of application and application forms for the particular role and how to prepare for and conduct interviews and selection centres to beat the competition.

Action point

Complete this exercise about developing your brand.

If you were a business with a strong brand what would: (a) be the key features and unique selling points of the business?; (b) be your brand values e.g. what type of attributes, strengths and characteristics would people associate with your brand?; and (c) how would you promote the business/brand?

Write these things down and use these to promote yourself as a jobseeker in applications and interviews etc.

It is essential to understand how to best market yourself and to create the best possible impression of your potential to be effective in the role. You may like to think of this as creating your own personal brand. In essence you need to know how to manage the application process – so ask yourself how do I get from here to there?

You can augment your career-development learning and work-based learning by thoroughly reflecting on your experiences and learning and writing this down after it happens so that you can reflect on it.

Reflection point

Think about the following: What happened today? What new knowledge or skill did I learn? What did I learn about myself? What would I do differently if I had to do that again?

Reflecting and writing in this way means you won't forget it and will help you to make claims about, articulate and provide evidence of your acquired skills, attributes and experience on CVs, application forms and in job interviews.

Where can I get career development support?

Career support is available from a variety of sources. These include from professionally qualified careers and employability advisers in colleges and universities. Commonly used higher education websites include www.prospects.ac.uk and www.target jobs.co.uk. Sector specific government websites such as www.justice.gov.uk/jobs can be very informative. Where available, other locally offered services such as Connexions Services could be useful to access. The National Careers Service is provided by the Government and offers online and telephone support – www.nationalcareersservice.direct.gov.uk/Pages/Home.aspx. It is also important to remember that others in your close network may also be valuable providers of information and advice, e.g. tutors, family, employers, neighbours and friends.

Who employs Criminal Justice graduates?

Major employers are central and local government, including: the Crown Prosecution Service, Home Office, Ministry of Justice, National Probation Service, Criminal Injuries Compensation Authority, Witness Care Unit, Her Majesty's Court Service, National Offender Management Service, charities, the Police and Prison Services, and other non-profit making organisations, including the NHS, educational institutions and Witness Support (who work with young offenders, families or victims of crime). Opportunities also increasingly exist in the private sector with organisations that operate Prison Services etc.

Criminal Justice graduates also work in a range of social welfare posts, such as mental health support workers, employment programme officers, drug rehabilitation workers, housing officers, outreach support roles such as homelessness officers and in refugee and victim support/counselling.

It is also important to remember that approximately half of all job vacancies for graduates are available to graduates of any academic subject discipline. In these cases the employer is more interested in the graduate's transferable graduate-level skills such as analysis, team working and problem solving and in their graduate-level employability skills like creativity, project management skills and emotional intelligence.

Making yourself employable

Motivation, enthusiasm, commitment – These are three key attributes that employers from all sectors regularly seek when they are recruiting students and graduates. Look through the information on websites, talk to someone working for an organisation or attend an employer talk offered at your college or university and you will regularly hear these words, regardless of which sector you would like to work in or what job you would like to do. Employers recruit graduates as a source of future talent and potential for their organisation, they want to recruit students who have the right attitude and personal characteristics, will become competent and effective and want to develop and progress within the company to help it grow.

How do I demonstrate motivation and enthusiasm?

There are various ways in which you can present these attributes in your application. First you can demonstrate this through the extra-curricular activities that you are involved in outside of university and employment. Employers are looking to recruit a well-rounded person with a mix of academic ability and personal skills and interests, and will actively look for evidence of these at each stage of the recruitment process. These extra-curricular activities can include individual hobbies, interests, participating in sports activities, community activities, membership of Student Union clubs and societies or other group-based activities. Undertaking *work experience* and *volunteering* are great ways to improve your employability and demonstrate motivation and enthusiasm both for developing yourself and learning about different occupational roles and sectors.

What type of work experience is available?

Work experience has become a general term, which incorporates a wide range of opportunities and experience. Ideally, the best way for employers to recruit a future graduate can be to see them in the workplace and observe how they perform undertaking tasks and managing deadlines or pressure on a daily basis. The following types of work experience can therefore be a way of securing a future graduate position at an organisation, including those in the Criminal Justice sector.

- *Year-long placements* – This type of placement can also be known as an industrial or thick-sandwich placement and the employer usually makes a salary payment. They can be a compulsory part of a university course but students on other courses may also have the option to take a year out from their studies and undertake a placement of this sort. This usually takes place between the second and third year of your course, i.e. before your final year of study.
- *Summer placements* – Increasingly the term *internship* is being used to describe placements that take place over the summer holidays usually for between 8 and 12 weeks. A definition of an internship is: *A short period of work-based professional experience during a degree programme.* Internships may be paid or unpaid, depending upon the employer's policy. They can be well-paid and, depending on the organisation and the sector, may only be available to students who have completed at least two years of their degree course. However a more recent trend is for some employers, for example those from the professional services sector, to offer short internships during the first year of study.
- *Work shadowing* – These opportunities are usually short-term and unpaid as you will not be undertaking a specific role in an organisation. The main activities include observing staff and gaining insight into a particular organisation. They can also be extremely useful in learning about a particular job role or function and for building up contacts and your network.
- *Part-time work* – These types of positions tend to be ongoing and you may, for example, be working for one or two days per week even during term time. These jobs may not necessarily be directly linked to your future career but they are still a great way to test yourself in different situations, develop skills, develop your organisational awareness and build up your CV.

Volunteering

Volunteering is a great way to develop skills, show your motivation, meet people and perhaps feel that you are giving something back to society. Many people may not consider volunteering as it is unpaid but it isn't important to future employers whether your work experience is paid or unpaid. In fact, volunteering looks good on your CV as it says something about you as a person, for example that you are prepared to work on an unpaid basis to support a project or community and develop personally. As with other work experience opportunities, it is a great way to improve your organisational and cultural awareness and build up contacts.

Volunteering will help you decide if it is the right career path for you, also the insider knowledge of the relevant agencies and the skills learnt will place you at an advantage in competing in the job market.

Action point

Consider you current commitment: list how many hours a week you spend:

- attending university, college, training
- on family commitments
- on employment commitments
- on study commitments.

How many hours would you be able to commit to volunteering a week?

What are your commitments this year?

- Are you planning on taking a year out?
- Are you planning on travelling through the summer?
  - These will not prevent you from volunteering but will help you identify your commitments.

Can you commit to at least one year's voluntary work?

Opportunities

Volunteering will provide you with a great opportunity of getting to know the organisation and roles first hand. You should be given high quality training to undertake the duties of a volunteer and offered the opportunity to access other training events available. So while developing your skills and knowledge base in taking advantage of the range of training on offer, you will also work closely with practitioners, work with those who have offended, develop one-to-one skills and demonstrate your ability to work as part of a team.

Opportunities for volunteering in the Criminal Justice sector include:

✓ Independent Monitoring Board members
✓ MAPPA lay advisers
✓ Restorative Justice panel members
✓ youth mentors
✓ prison visitors
✓ faith-based volunteers involved in prison, 'through the prison gate', and in the community
✓ prison visitor centres and children's area facilitators
✓ appropriate and trusted adults
✓ victim/offender mediation
✓ volunteers engaged in work in the National Offender Management Service reducing re-offending pathways: accommodation; education, training and employment; health; drugs and alcohol
✓ finance benefit and debt; children and families; attitudes, thinking and behaviour
✓ work with high risk of harm offenders.

How to find work experience opportunities

• *Contacting your careers service or centre* would be an important first step. Often they will have lots of information about employers willing to consider this and also may advertise volunteering opportunities on vacancy lists and websites.

- *Company websites* – the information is usually in the *careers* section. It is important to check the closing dates for more structured opportunities and programmes such as year-long and summer placements as you may need to apply for these a long time ahead and often as early as the beginning of the penultimate academic year.
- *University subject departments* – some departments will have dedicated work-based learning staff to support you in finding a placement, particularly a year-long or industrial placement. These staff are often part of a work-based learning unit or office.
- *Speculative applications* – these applications are made when you are not responding to an advertised job/opportunity advert but are proactively contacting an organisation to explore the possibility of securing a job or work experience opportunity. For this process it is vital to ensure that you have an effective and up to date CV and covering letter, so contact your careers service/centre for support or look online. In addition, you should also consider SMEs (Small to Medium-Sized Enterprises with fewer than 250 employees) in addition to larger, more traditional graduate employers. SMEs make up the vast majority of employers in the UK, so are a very good source of opportunities for you. To find out about SMEs you can ask your careers service/centre, look in employer directories that you can access in public libraries, contact the local Chamber of Commerce or contact professional institutions or associations.
- *Use contacts* – you may already be working part-time in an organisation, so ask about other opportunities such as year-long and summer placements.

Action point

Websites are a free resource. Use search engines to find related useful sites. Why not ask people working in the profession for advice about where the best sites are and also ask them if they were you how would they approach this?

What will I get out of work experience?

Benefits of work experience:

- get hands on experience in possible future job roles;
- provides relevant information about future careers;
- provides opportunities for networking and information about job opportunities and employers' recruitment methods. It's a great way to build up contacts;
- you may get paid;
- builds up your CV and provides examples to use in applications and at interview;
- provides experience of a professional working environment and improves your organisational awareness;
- builds your confidence;
- you will develop a range of skills, even if it's not entirely related to a future graduate role and it shows that you are a motivated person who wants to develop.

How to make the most of work experience?

- See it as an opportunity to gain experience, information and to test you in a different situation or role – a positive approach would be best so get involved, have a can-do attitude and ask questions.
- It is important to 'sell' these experiences on your CV and application forms. The experience is great but it is equally, if not more, important to be able to tactically highlight it on your CV and at interviews. As well as thinking of the day-to-day tasks that you undertook also focus on your responsibilities and the skills that you developed, e.g. communication, teamwork, organisation, problem-solving, adaptability. Be able to explain how you approached a task or problem and what worked well.
- Networking/contacts – use the opportunity to build up a range of contacts that can provide information on the particular job, organisation and possible opportunities, and also the recruitment practices that the company uses, as well as providing a possible reference in the future. A useful

consequence of establishing a network is that you may also find that you are informed of or considered for future job openings.

- Speak to a Careers Adviser or an academic tutor with experience of the sector or profession for advice on how you can best utilise these experiences to improve your CV and the implications for your possible career options.

Reflection point

Reflect on your experience – What went well? Would you do anything differently if you had another opportunity? Are there any gaps in your skills or attributes – which you will need, in your future career? Will this experience help you in your future career? Be positive and have a can-do attitude.

Work experience and the Criminal Justice sector

Employers in the Criminal Justice sector, like most employers in other sectors, will look for evidence from you of knowledge and understanding of job roles and the extent to which you have considered aspects of the role and the suitability to your skills, attributes, motivations and aspirations. One of the best, if not the best way, of demonstrating these things is undertaking work-related or work-based experience. Examples of work-related experience include simulations/role play within your academic programme and working on sector related projects or research. As explained before, examples of work-based experience in the Criminal Justice sector typically include work placements and/or internships, which can vary in length from a few weeks to a year. Criminal Justice employers value this type of experience so much that those without it are highly likely to be disadvantaged and less competitive when applying for jobs. Because of this you should set out to make the most of all opportunities that might be presented to you and if they are not presented to you then you should proactively set about securing both work-related and work-based experiences for yourself. There are a variety of people who will help you to do this, including your academic tutors, work experience and placements staff in your faculty or school, the university careers service/centre, the Student Union, student societies, professional associations, charities, and friends and relatives etc. When conducting your research and preparing for your experience, you should check the 'terms and conditions' and importantly the nature of the support available and any rewards e.g. payment, allowance, financial bursary etc. A range of paid and voluntary work opportunities exists, including work with offenders, Criminal Justice agencies and victims of crime. Social work and community education departments based in local authorities and not-for-profit organisations also offer relevant opportunities.

Action point

Look at the reflection point below. Make a plan to properly understand the differences between larger and smaller organisations and how workplaces can be transformed by working in teams or independently. Why not write to professionals who are working in different settings and organisations and ask them to describe what it is like and why they like it. Alternatively look for YouTube videos where people describe their roles.

Reflection point

It would be wise to think about the organisation, client group and type of Criminal Justice environment you are interested in. For example, whether your preference is to work for a large formal organisation or a smaller community-based group or charity and also what type of client you prefer to work with. Here, for example, you may have preferences for working with a varied group of people, with young or older people, with people that have particular needs or support, such as those with certain dependencies like drugs or alcohol. It is important to plan how you will achieve your experience and how you could, for example, get involved with local charities, support groups or initiatives aimed at supporting offenders and/or reducing the risk of offending. Focussing on your professional preferences will allow you to prioritise and target specific employers and voluntary organisations and thus give you the most personally valuable experience you can get.

What skills and competencies will Criminal Justice employers expect?

Common skills-sets are required regardless of the level of education and at what point you are entering the profession. It is essential to reflect on these and to know which ones you can say you possess and be able to provide evidence to back up your claims. The following skills are important: communication, empathy, resilience, organisation and team working.

By studying for a degree and becoming a graduate you are developing a very wide range of skills and competencies. These are often referred to as graduate skills and/or transferable skills. These include 'hard' technical subject related skills and 'soft' interpersonal skills. Employers commonly demand applicants to clearly articulate evidence of both hard skills such as those associated with your subject of study and particularly soft skills, such as approachability and/or leadership: this is during the application stage, on the application form itself and also during the other selection processes like interviews and assessment centre activities.

Graduate skills contribute to developing 'graduateness'. Employers want graduate applicants to explain how they are differentiated from non-graduates and a sound way of doing this is to refer to the set of skills you have developed as a result of your degree-level studies. It is very important to know what employers want and the Confederation of British Industry (CBI) has identified seven key employability skills sought by employers. They are self-management, team working, business and customer awareness, problem-solving, communication and literacy, application of numeracy and application of information technology. Employers also want an enterprising mind-set and a positive attitude.

Graduates typically possess the following skills: analytical skills, written and verbal communication, team work, numerical reasoning, information communications technology, organisation, planning, working to deadlines, self-motivation and working autonomously. Graduates who have studied Criminal Justice will have developed a good understanding of criminal law and the Criminal Justice System, the effects and consequences of criminal behaviour (including societal, social and personal aspects), critical thinking, the effects on victims and responses to crime and deviance. Alongside the generic graduate skills mentioned above, graduates of Criminal Justice will also have developed skills such as generating, interpreting and evaluating data, forming measured and reasoned arguments and coming to ethical decisions and judgements.

It is worth considering in further detail the generic graduate employability skills identified by the CBI:

Self-management is about managing your time, reflecting on and assessing your performance to identify strengths and areas for further development and accepting responsibility.

Action point

Activities to develop and provide evidence for self-management include: positions of responsibility in student societies, balancing varied activities and commitments alongside your studies (e.g. running a family), being pro-active by arranging work experience placements, work shadowing or a mentor.

Team work is about achieving something with others where there is a shared sense of purpose and where there are agreed inter-dependent complementary roles. It involves accepting responsibility, being willing to play a specified team role, appreciating and supporting others and being reliable.

> ### Action point
>
> Activities to develop and provide evidence for team work include: team activities like sports, drama, fundraising, volunteering, running events, charitable activities, participating in group subject-based projects, part-time work or work placements.

Business and customer awareness includes having knowledge of how businesses and organisations function, the environment in which they operate, how customer satisfaction is achieved and how your role impacts on the objectives or success of the business/organisation.

> ### Action point
>
> Activities to develop and provide evidence for business and customer awareness include: being employed (perhaps in a customer-facing role), running a small business or social enterprise, holding a sales or fundraising position where targets had to be met, managing a budget for a student society or group, being involved in enterprise, small business or investment clubs.

Problem solving is about recognising and dealing with problems, discovering and implementing solutions.

> ### Action point
>
> Activities to develop and provide evidence for problem solving include: remembering a time when a difficult issue or situation arose, identifying how you analysed things in a systematic way to target the problematic element(s), how you decided to tackle these, what actions you took, whether these were successful and reflecting on what, if anything, you might do differently if the scenario happened again.

Communication and literacy includes listening to others, requesting information and getting your message across. Having strong written and verbal communication skills is essential for graduate employment. Being a strong communicator will allow you to articulate your skills to employers.

Action point

Activities to develop and provide evidence for communication and literacy include: the varied pieces of work submitted as part of your studies. Work-related or voluntary roles where regular communication with others was essential (e.g. via email, face-to-face or over the telephone), any customer service roles particularly where you might have provided advice or dealt with customer complaints.

Application of numeracy includes the analysis and management of numbers, statistics or other quantitative data. Having numerical skills is attractive across a range of occupations and therefore should be emphasised.

Action point

Activities to develop and provide evidence for application of numerical skills include: working with statistics or financial data in part-time jobs or work experience, keeping the accounts for a student society, voluntary or charity group, managing a small business.

Application of information technology is about basic use of computers and applications like writing documents, email, using the Internet and optimising social media and most graduates will be expected to have these skills.

There are many other 'soft' skills and attributes that are often mentioned as attractive by employers. Some of these that employers within the Criminal Justice sector might regard as important include:

Active or attentive listening – an ability to hear what people are actually saying not what you think they should be saying;

Measured/balanced decision-making – an ability to evenly and fairly evaluate a situation or information and make an ethical decision that takes into account all the facts and aspects available;

Attention to detail – being thorough and rarely making mistakes with, for example, data;

Commitment to the task or job – an ability to stay focussed and motivated to get things done;

Consistency and reliability – an ability to deliver what is required time after time;

Empathetic approach – an ability to see a situation from the viewpoint of the person concerned, to understand what they may be feeling and experiencing;

Emotional control – an ability to be measured and objective when faced with emotional or stressful situations, not to act in a knee-jerk or overly emotional way;

Tenacity – an ability to be persistent and focussed on the task or job when faced with obstacles or barriers;

Personal accountability – a willingness and ability to be take responsibility for your own actions and decisions, not passing the buck or making excuses.

Thinking about your competencies is also essential. The Ministry of Justice (www.justice.gov.uk – 2014), for example, has developed a competency and qualities framework (CQF) for the Prison Service. The CQF has been developed by the Prison Service to reflect: Prison Service values; the law; current and prospective business requirements; the Prison Service's commitment to equality and diversity; Professional Skills for Government (PSG) core skills and leadership. The framework consists of twelve behavioural competences, grouped under three headings: working professionally; working with others and working to achieve results. The 12 competencies are:

1 WORKING PROFESSIONALLY

1A *Achieving a safe and secure environment*: promotes and contributes to an orderly, safe and secure environment; both within own unit/establishment and across the Prison Service.

1B *Showing resilience*: is consistently motivated, committed and able to perform duties in all situations.

1C *Acting with integrity*: consistently acts in a principled, open and conscientious manner, and challenges unacceptable behaviour.

1D *Respecting others*: promotes equality of opportunity; treating all people with fairness, dignity and respect. Challenges discriminatory behaviour, and upholds and fosters diversity.

2 WORKING WITH OTHERS

2A *Persuading and influencing*: persuades, influences and listens to others, using reason and co-operation to reach agreement.

2B *Building relationships and team working*: Supporting each other and building relationships to achieve common goals.

2C *Communicating effectively*: communicates and receives ideas, views and information to achieve understanding.

2D *Caring*: shows concern for colleagues, prisoners, and others, recognising their needs and providing practical support.

3 WORKING TO ACHIEVE RESULTS

3A *Problem solving and decision-making*: gathers information from a range of sources. Analyses information to identify problems and issues and makes effective decisions.

3B *Organising and maximising performance*: plans and supervises activities and resources to maximise performance.
3C *Embracing change*: acknowledges the need to achieve positive change, and challenges existing practices.
3D *Developing self and others*: takes ownership of personal development and encourages and supports the development of others.

Employers use competences to assist them to define what an employee should be doing in their role and how they should do it to meet the needs of their role. Competencies are based on how employees carry out the duties and tasks their job involves.

Competencies focus on the things that contribute to an employee's and organisation's success. They communicate and explain achievements and can be used to identify development needs or gaps in people resources. Competencies help organisations perform well, so knowing your competencies and being able to provide evidence for them is a useful and necessary tactic.

Reflection point

Imagine you are asked to make claims about the competencies you possess. Make a list of what you would say with examples of situations where you have needed to use the competency. Also make a list of your strongest competencies and write down a rank order explaining why they are the strongest. Another idea is to ask someone else what competencies they think you possess.

Making sure you understand what skills and competencies an employer in the Criminal Justice sectors requires is clearly important in helping to make a successful application and achieve your objective of getting the job. For example, the civil service has a major long-term programme to make sure civil servants have the right blend of knowledge and skills to deliver their roles successfully. This is called Building Professional Skills for Government. The core skills are leadership, project and people management, communications and marketing, strategic thinking, analysis and use of evidence, and financial management.

Action point

Comparing your skill-set with frameworks like this one can make you better informed about the requirements of the role, can help you assess your suitability and assist you to identify gaps in your skills profile thus making you better prepared and hopefully more confident.

Resilience – a key skill for working in the Criminal Justice sector

People who work in the Criminal Justice sector are likely to encounter people who may feel vulnerable, alienated, marginalised, victimised and angry. Such people may be very challenging to work with. The ability to be resilient and mentally tough will therefore be important. Resilience at work can be described as having the attributes, personal capacity and ability to remain focussed and on-track with whatever is normal or expected in the face of stress or commonplace or unusual difficulties. Resilience is about seeing a piece of work or task through to a conclusion without being diverted from the main purpose. When working in demanding roles with people who might cause psychological distress to others around them, being resilient is important to prevent the damaging effects of such distress. For those working in the Criminal Justice sector possessing some or a lot of resilience can be important. Resilience can be learned and is not necessarily innate.

Understanding the organisation you want to work for

It is extremely important to be able to develop insight into the organisation and sector you are considering as an employment option – how it functions, the environment it operates in and additionally who its clients, customers and service users are.

This is important because by developing your organisational awareness you will be able to make better informed decisions about the type of work you wish to secure and the sort of employer that might suit you best. By ensuring that your own values and ethics match those of an organisation, you are taking a significant step towards employment that will be more likely to be motivating and rewarding. Also, at both application and interview stages, employers including those from the Criminal Justice sector will be looking for evidence that you understand their organisation. They want to recruit people who care about what the organisation does and who have considered whether they will fit in well and be able to add value to help the organisation meet the objectives it has set.

To assess this, employers will typically ask questions such as:

- Why do you want to enter this profession/sector?
- What do you know about our organisation?
- What are our main services/outputs?
- What do you think the job you would be doing involves?
- What are the challenges facing our profession/sector at this time?
- What changes have there been in our profession/sector recently?

- What other organisations operate in our sector? Would you regard them as competitors? What are the differences between them and us?
- Who are our clients?
- How do you keep up to date with current issues in the sector?

> **Action point**
>
> There is no substitute for research and talking to professionals doing the jobs. Make a plan perhaps stretching over a year or more of how you will familiarise yourself with job roles and the sector. Make a list of the resources you will access and how you will get hold of them. Always be willing to ask for help from someone on the inside of the profession.

There are many resources available to you to help you research an organisation and the sector in which it operates. One of the first places to start is the organisation's website. It's likely that you will find lots of relevant information here about the history, function, mission, structure, values and culture of the organisation. Take a look at the 'working with us' pages for insight into what they are looking for in their employees and volunteers and consider if you are a good match for them – assessing whether your values and motivations align with theirs. You may find information published for stake holders (such as funding bodies, government departments, community groups and professional associations) particularly useful. Read recent annual reports with details of performance to analyse key trends for the organisation. These are often very useful to help you produce a well-informed interview.

You should also carefully analyse the job description and person specification for the role you are interested in. This should help you to identify how to best demonstrate that you meet all of the requirements for the role and to produce a suitably tailored application.

Don't be afraid to contact the organisation directly for further information. Employers often value candidates who show a genuine interest by asking for a short meeting or telephone conversation to discuss the role and support their research prior to applying. You should think about which person in the organisation can provide you with the answers you need. This may typically be someone from the human resources department or could be someone who acts as the professional lead or team manager for a particular function or team. If you are unsure who to contact and how best to do it, you can always phone or email a general enquiries line if there is one or contact the reception and politely ask for some assistance. Asking the following question would be appropriate 'I am thinking of applying for post X and I have some questions about the post. Who would you recommend I speak to about this and how should I go about contacting them?' Just be sure to carefully work out what you want to ask and why you are asking the questions. Check that the answers to any questions you want to ask are not within the information the employer has sent out or posted online already, as this would indicate that you have not read this information carefully enough and that you might lack organisation and an eye for detail.

Social networks can also be a great way to find out accurate, up to date information about an organisation. For example, you can research an organisation on LinkedIn and make contact with current employees to help you to develop insight into what it's like to work there and the sector in general. Twitter is also a useful tool by following people who are posting relevant information about their employer or industry. Similarly, a company's pages on Facebook can have valuable information for anyone looking to build a profile of the organisation. In the Criminal Justice sector you may find that these sources of information are significantly more limited than if you were applying for posts in the private commercial sector. However, this is worth exploring as you might uncover something that makes a major difference to your application.

Equally, employers are looking for candidates who can demonstrate that they understand the environment that the organisation operates in. Specific research into the sector or industry can be done by keeping updated with industry publications and professional bodies. You may also want to look at recent market research reports for information on developments, trends, key players and current issues. These are all good topics for interview questions.

Finally, a good grasp of professional issues will ensure that a potential employer views you as being professionally connected and aware. You should be able to analyse and evaluate the impact of issues in areas such as politics, public policy, the economy, society and technology on the organisation. Following the organisation in local and even national press should give you good insight and support your understanding of your chosen organisation and industry. Aim to understand the organisation in its external context.

Am I motivated towards a career of public service?

Public services can have the characteristic of a public benefit or good associated with them, i.e. something that is available to everyone and that does not usually have competitors. Such services tend to be those regarded as morally necessary for a functioning society, helping people to live their lives. Law enforcement and social services would commonly be included within a list of public services. Obviously in the main these services do not involve the production of 'things', e.g. consumable goods. They often demand high levels of training, education and skills from those who provide services and often attract people with what might be called a public service ethos, who wish to work for and provide services and support for the wider public or community through their job.

In most developed countries public services are still organised and provided by local or national government. This is known as the public sector, where making a profit is not usually an objective, with the significant exceptions being the USA and the UK, where privately organised and delivered services and support are more developed and common. Where this is the case, privately provided public services are often very formally regulated and are being provided because the public authorities/government do not have the funds to provide services and/or are politically driven to create provision and policy that includes private providers. An example of an established private provider in the UK Criminal Justice sector is G4S, which provides the following services: custodial and detention services, probation and security, Police support services, children's services, electronic monitoring and prisoner escorting and court custody services.

Alongside this trend to privatise services is the attempt by central government in the UK to promote and encourage charities to take a more active role in providing services and support. This has in recent times become a part of the government rhetoric on Criminal Justice. Only weeks after the UK Coalition Government came to power in 2010, the Justice Secretary, Kenneth Clarke, publically highlighted the growth in the prison population, the rising rate of re-offending and the ineffectiveness of short sentences. He said: 'We want a far more constructive approach. The voluntary and private sectors will be crucial to our success. We want to make far better use of their enthusiasm and expertise to get offenders away from the revolving door of crime and prison'. However government funds made available to charities to support their work have not been forthcoming. Clinks (2013), the umbrella group of Criminal Justice charities and voluntary organisations, published a detailed survey of its 450 members in May 2012. The survey reported 95 per cent of organisations had, or expected to have, a reduction in income, 77 per cent are using their reserves to survive and 55 per cent had made staff redundancies. The survey concluded that many organisations were experiencing acute demand for services with decreased resources. There was a higher level and more complex type of need in users. The devaluing of services by using volunteers was a concern and service users were being impacted by funding cuts despite the organisations' best efforts.

The privatisation of the Criminal Justice sector commonly means a move to more private ownership and control of Criminal Justice services. This term is often used to describe contracting out of services, for example Prison Services provided by private providers. Much is written about the Criminal Justice System, which demonstrates the on-going debate over who should manage prisons, oversee offenders, and, even who should police the streets. Having an awareness of the issues and being able to talk about these in applications and during interviews is important.

Thinking about what is important to you when choosing a career is essential. You may want to consider the perceived relative benefits of working for a private or public employer such as salary, holidays, training support, equal opportunities, the chances of career development and promotion and job security. Researching the terms and conditions attached to each job will uncover this information, which will allow comparisons to be made. If you want a career of public service where contributing to the public good is important and giving back to the community are reasons that motivate you, then you will need to weigh all these factors up. You will need to decide whether these things are achievable regardless of whether the provider of the service, and therefore your employer, is a public or private organisation. If you have a preference for one or the other then this should inform your decision about which employer you choose. It is important that you reflect on your values, beliefs and preferences and assess what you want your career to stand for and decide upon the type of sector you want to work in.

The hidden jobs market

Not all jobs are openly advertised, in fact organisations are under no legal obligation to advertise their positions externally. This means that when you look at job postings online or in the newspapers you are only seeing a fraction of the real job market, or the 'open job market' as it is called. What you don't see are the hundreds of other jobs that are offered and accepted through other means and never advertised openly, this is often referred to as the 'hidden job market'. This does not mean these opportunities are closed to you, just that you may have to be more aware and creative when it comes to uncovering job vacancies.

Networking is the key to opening the door to the hidden job market and it really is easier than you might think. Here are some suggestions to get your network started and noticed by future employers.

Get out there! Find out what events are coming up in and around your area where individuals and employers you would like to work for may be in attendance. These may be graduate recruitment fairs, conferences, open meetings, seminars and talks and can even be social events.

Once you are at an event make the most of it. Ensure you have done your research on the organisations you are interested in working for and go prepared to discuss your motivations and to find out how job vacancies may come up. Employers are impressed by people who are truly passionate about working for them, so demonstrating this knowledge is an effective way to engage them in conversation. Gaining an email address or further contact details from anyone you meet that may be useful in the future is essential. Always ensure you follow up any useful meetings or discussions you have had with an email or phone call, thanking people for their time. These people can be added to your contact list, which is an integral part of building your personal network. In the future you may want to ask these contacts for an 'information interview', this is when you spend a bit of time picking the brains of your contacts, gaining some useful knowledge about an industry or career path.

Staying up to date and in touch with a careers service/centre that might organise specific networking events with possible employer organisations is important. Making contacts at events like these is easier because the employers attend with the express purpose of meeting new contacts and even new potential employees so your task should be more straightforward. So ask about and trawl through events calendars to keep up to date.

As mentioned before, social media can be extremely useful and can help you access the hidden job market. You can use social media to follow organisations and even individuals working in the sector you are hoping to go in to.

LinkedIn is the leading professional network on the Internet. Your LinkedIn profile acts as a CV and you can connect with individuals and organisations to increase your network and gain insight into your industry. There are even a number of sector specific groups on the website, which you can join and where you will meet other professionals and make some great connections.

To find out more about joining and utilising LinkedIn check out the instructional videos here: www.learn.linkedin.com/students/step-1.

So, here are some of things you need to do to uncover those hidden job opportunities:

- keep your eye out for events you can meet people and network at;
- use social media, especially LinkedIn, to make contacts;
- make use of your contacts to gain valuable information and insights into organisations you want to target;
- make a good, well informed impression and you might just get offered a placement, internship or even a job.

Being proactive rather than reactive could be the key to success. As well as meeting prospective employers through networking, online or at events, you can also promote yourself through a speculative application. This involves sending a CV along with a covering letter to an employer who may not be currently advertising any placements, internships or job vacancies. This is of course speculative so you don't know what might come out of this endeavour, in many senses it is a gamble and you are hoping to strike lucky. If an employer is impressed by your proactivity and confidence and likes your CV and covering letter they may contact you for a further discussion. You may not be offered a job straightaway but you may be considered for future positions or a position could be created for you. Here are some tips to make a great first impression and optimise your chances through speculative applications:

- Always make sure your CV and covering letter are targeted to a specific role and the organisation it is being sent to. Always research the target organisation thoroughly using the techniques discussed in this chapter.

- Always get a named contact. Your application form will make more of an impact and go to the right person if you make sure it is addressed to the appropriate person. You can always call up an organisation to ask for a named contact.
- Follow up your speculative application with a phone call or email. This will demonstrate that you are genuinely interested and enthusiastic in working for them.

Selection processes

Across the Criminal Justice sector the use of certain selection methods and techniques is common. Always ensure that you closely match the requirements of the job description and person specification. These tell you exactly what is required and you should look very carefully at each aspect and element and connect your qualifications, skills, competencies, behaviours and experiences to them. The selection methods and techniques include:

- *Application forms* – these will often ask you to provide comments and evidence of your competencies and increasingly behaviours, e.g. how good are you at things, how well you perform certain skills and how you react and manage situations, tasks and challenges. These forms can be completed on paper or electronically and often stipulate a word-count, so it is important to adhere to these. Reading the instructions very carefully is important as selectors will take a dim view of applicants that don't and particularly those who state that they have an eye for detail and can follow instructions! Always ask someone else to proofread your application for any mistakes.
- *Selection centres* – these normally consist of a number of different tasks aimed to test your suitability for the post being applied for. These can include *psychometric tests*, which will test your (a) numerical ability, e.g. interpreting data and statistics often presented in tables, charts and lists (b) verbal ability, e.g. interpreting written information and (c) diagrammatic or spatial ability, e.g. interpreting shapes and often working out how a flattened shape would look as a 3D shape. Other psychometric tests can focus on

becoming employable

personality and will test how you respond to certain questions and situations and evaluate your preferences.

- *Interviews* – these can be part of the selection centre or can be separate. Interviews can be conducted on a one-to-one basis or with a panel of interviewers. A panel might typically consist of two to three interviewers or could be more. Each interviewer will ask different types of questions and they will all decide on the applicant's suitability for the post.

A useful method to help you manage applications and interview questions is the *STAR* technique, this includes:

- *Situation* – what was the situation? Briefly describe the context.
- *Task* – describe what the problem was or what you needed to achieve.
- *Action* – what did you do, how did you do it and what skills did you use?
- *Result* – what did you achieve, what was the outcome and what did you learn? Make sure it shows you in a good light, even if the overall result was not a success.

General advice for all selection processes is always be sure why you are applying for the post. Know as much as you can about yourself and the organisation you are applying to, always do some in-depth planning and preparation and tell the truth on applications forms. Make confident claims about your skills, experience and suitability and always back up your claims with evidence. Be sure to say why you want the job and why you think you are a strong candidate. Think about the type of questions you might be asked and rehearse your answers. Why not ask your career service or a friend to conduct a mock interview. This will make you feel more confident and relaxed during the process. Think about questions you might have about the organisation as they will almost certainly ask if you have any. Common interview questions include:

1   Tell me about yourself.
2   Why have you applied for this particular role?
3   Why do you want to work for this organisation?

4   What skills can you bring to the job?
5   What do you consider to be your greatest achievement and why?
6   What are your views on ...? (current issue related to the industry/sector)

Chapter summary

This chapter has covered some of the essential elements of becoming employable. There is much to think about and the emphasis is clearly on you being, among other things, proactive, organised and confident. Being honest, reflective and willing to get to know yourself is essential, as is understanding as much as possible about the opportunities, organisations and sector you apply to. Getting a job is a job in itself!

Top tips

- reflect
- record
- remember
- make claims about your skills and experiences
- provide evidence to back up your claims
- get work experience
- do an internship
- do some volunteering
- use the careers service
- investigate company websites
- use your academic department
- make speculative applications
- use your contacts/networks

- do your research into a potential employer
- use the company website
- business libraries can be useful
- don't be afraid to ask questions of the employer
- use social networks
- ask someone else to proofread your application forms.

Work experience

- enhances your CV
- develops new skills
- helps you to make an informed career choice
- provides an opportunity to meet a wide range of people
- allows you to make a difference to the community you live in and to the lives of those people you support.

Some useful websites

- www.prospects.ac.uk (A careers information advice and job vacancies site for graduates)
- www.justice.gov.uk/jobs (Information about Criminal Justice in the UK)
- www.nationalcareersservice.direct.gov.uk/Pages/Home.aspx (Careers information and advice for all)
- www.targetjobs.co.uk (Careers information, advice and job vacancies for graduates)

Recommended reading

There are a wealth of career information guides and books available. By researching the above websites you will be able to locate the most suitable for you. We would recommend however that you look at the Brilliant Careers guides by Pearson.

References

Clinks (2013) The State of the Sector VCS in the Economic Downturn. Retrieved from www.clinks.org/eco-downturn (accessed 27 May 2014)

Law, B. and Watts, A. G. (1977) *Schools, Careers and Community: A study of some approaches to careers education in schools*. London: Church Information Office

Ministry of Justice (2008) Competencies and Qualities Framework. Retrieved from www.justice.gov.uk/downloads/jobs/hmps-compe tence-framework.pdf (accessed 27 May 2014)

Working in probation

Introduction to the Probation Service

The Probation Service is an integral component of the Criminal Justice Systems in the United Kingdom. It provides an essential service to the courts and manages those individuals who have been made subject to community supervision and suspended sentence orders or those sentenced to a term of imprisonment and subject to licensing conditions in the community. In the past probation was seen as an alternative to imprisonment but recent decades have seen it become a sentence in its own right. The staff who work in these services are known as Probation Officers or Probation Service Officers in England, Wales and Northern Ireland and as Criminal Justice social workers and Criminal Justice Officers in Scotland. The majority of the probation staffs are based in community teams; however there are also probation staff in the courts, the hostels and the prisons so it offers you a wide range of employment opportunities. The Service has a commitment to *multi-agency working* and *partnerships*: this provides probation staff with the opportunity to work closely with other agencies. This means that not only would you be working with highly skilled and qualified colleagues from within the service but you would be working in a multi-agency setting with individual organisations from the *voluntary*, *private* and *statutory* sector. This would include organisations from the substance misuse services, the employment and training sector or the statutory agencies, which would include Social Services, the Police Service or the Prisons.

Reflection point

Take a look at the book *Multi-agency working in Criminal Justice* edited by Pycroft and Gough. This text will give you practical insight into multi-agency working.

Probation Service Officer, 'I wish I'd known when going into Criminal Justice that I think the best skill you can have, and are required to use on a daily basis, is to be able to network effectively with different people from a variety of organisations. Working in Criminal Justice, you often need to liaise with the Police, Social Care (services), CPS, housing providers, drugs/alcohol agencies etc. and you often need to 'pull in a favour' or negotiate with someone in order to make arrangements.'

Action point

Revisit Chapter 2 and read how the Probation Service fits in
with the Criminal Justice Service.

Having read Chapter 2 you will have an understanding of the
role of the Service in the Criminal Justice System. This chapter
will begin by providing *a brief overview* of the Probation Service
in England and Wales and consider the *aims and values* that
underpin the functions of the service. *Key figures* will be provided
in relation to the number of staff employed and the number of
orders managed by the Service. The chapter will then move on
to consider the *functions* of the service and the *roles* and *careers*,
this will take us through the *entry requirements*, *skills* and
training opportunities. Within this chapter the careers discussed
will be the *Probation Service Officer*, *Probation Officer* and
Senior Probation Officer. These careers have been chosen because
they provide a natural career progression through the service.
There will be practical guidance throughout the chapter and
reflection and action points will give you the opportunity to begin
to think about developing a career in the Probation Service. There
are also some comments from practitioners working in the field
to give you some tips about the role.

The last part of the chapter will consider the *Northern Ireland
Probation Service* and the *Scottish Probation Service*. Given the
roles and functions of the probation practitioner are similar, we
will not duplicate the material but discuss areas of difference.

Reflection point

It is very important to acknowledge that as we write this
book the service in *England* and *Wales* is experiencing a
period of rapid change. We do know that practitioners of
Probation Service Officer and Probation Officer grade will

work in both the National Probation Service and The Community Rehabilitation Companies, we also know that the National Offender Management Service has made a commitment to continue with a training plan for practitioners of Probation Service Officer grades to become qualified Probation Officers; what we do not know is the format of these arrangements. Therefore this chapter is written to be as broad as possible.

To understand the Probation Service's current positioning within the Criminal Justice System, it is important to have some knowledge and understanding of where it has come from and the implications of these changes. This chapter provides a very brief overview but does not seek to put these changes into any meaningful context or summarise its development succinctly.

Action point

You would benefit from reading texts such as Mair and Burke (2011), which can provide an in-depth discussion about the different phases that the Probation Service has experienced.

Reflection point

We need to acknowledge that the term 'offender' is used, one that does not sit comfortably with many practitioners due to the negative labelling. It is used because it is a label that has been ascribed to an individual who has committed an offence, been apprehended by the Police, charged by the Crown Prosecution Service and appeared before the courts and sentenced accordingly.

The Probation Service in England and Wales

The National Probation Service has evolved over a period of over 100 years and throughout this period the Service's aims and values have altered and developed from a period of *advise, assist and befriend* to the current focus of *rehabilitation, enforcement and public protection*. The Service's values have been influenced by religious ideals, scientific advancements, anti-discriminatory principles and evidence based practice. It has also been influenced by a range of political agendas of the day and a range of legislation, which has seen the introduction of new orders and influences on practice.

- The 1991 Criminal Justice Act was a radical piece of legislation, which saw a raft of changes: the Probation Order became a sentence in its own right; new orders were introduced such as Community Service, day centres, bail hostels and a range of conditions in Probation Orders.
- These changes began to see the Service move from a social work ethos to a more Justice-orientated focus.
- In 1992 national standards were introduced and with them the introduction of cash-linked targets.
- The 1990s saw a change in the professional qualifications from social work to a more justice-oriented probation qualification.
- There was growth in the 'What Works' movement and the introduction of Evidence Based Effective Practice and accredited programmes.
- In 2001 the Probation Service was centralised and became a National Probation Service and in 2004 the Probation Service

was joined with the Prison Service to become the National Offender Management Service (NOMS).

- This saw the introduction of the Offender Management Model, which provides guidance on an end-to-end seamless sentence for offenders. Practitioners became identified as Offender Managers and supported by Offender Supervisors (although never lost the term Probation Officer).
- Following the 2007 Offender Management Act, the 42 probation areas became 35 self-governing probation trusts.

Reflection point

The Transforming Rehabilitation Agenda has been introduced, which changes the way the probation services are delivered. The services to offenders will be provided by the National Probation Service and 21 Community Rehabilitation Companies, and these are the agencies you will be approaching for employment.

The National Probation Service will continue to provide a service to the courts and manage those assessed as higher risk to the public, while those assessed as lower risk offenders will be managed by the Community Rehabilitation Companies.

The National Probation Service has clear aims to guide its practitioners and inform the wider community of what it does. It is important when considering a career in any service that you understand its *aims* and the *value base* that guides practice. This shows a wider understanding of the work the organisation carries out and the focus of its organisation and workforce. This will help you to assess whether you can match these and whether you still wish to come into the service. It is important to look at the individual Mission Statements of the areas you may be looking to work in as they have varying statements. These aims and values here are general and guide the service.

Aims of the National Probation Service as identified
by *A New Choreography* (NPS 2001)

- protecting the Public
- reducing re-offending
- the proper punishment of offenders
- ensuring offenders awareness of the effects of their crimes on its victims and the public
- the Rehabilitation of offenders.

Values as stated in Bold Steps, the NPS business plan
2004

- staff and partnership colleagues are the organisation's greatest asset;
- victim awareness and empathy are central to what we do;
- public protection is of paramount importance;
- law enforcement to ensure compliance wherever possible or, where necessary, to take appropriate and timely action;
- working positively to achieve the restoration and rehabilitation of offenders;
- basing all practice on evidence of 'What Works';
- a commitment to continuous improvement;
- openness and transparency in what we do;
- responding and learning to work positively with difference in order to value and achieve diversity;
- problem-solving to resolve conflict and 'do business';
- partnership, using a collaborative approach to add value to the capacity of the NPD to achieve expected outcomes;
- better quality services – ensuring that the public receive effective services at the best price.

You will note that these values read more like a statement of intent and that is because as an organisation, the National Probation Service has never formally identified its own values but rather drawn its values from the organisations it is associated with. For example, in the beginning the Service would have held the values of saving souls and this would have been the missionary ideals of the Church of England. Then in the latter part of the twentieth century the Service had adopted the social work values based on those of anti-discrimination.

Action point

Take a look at the local probation area you are considering or intending to apply to and look at the mission statement they have issued. What are the values outlined there?

Reflection point

Think about how your values may or may not fit in with those outlines by the Service. Remember, values are individual and personal commitments to what you believe to be morally right, and you need to understand what it is you believe in and what you believe to be right courses of action.

When you begin to consider a career in the National Probation Service or the Community Rehabilitation Companies, it is important to consider some key figures such as the high numbers of staff employed within the current structure, these numbers will continue to be essential to the effective management of offenders. Take a look at the key figures of probation and although the caseload is declining year on year it is important to acknowledge the high number of cases that proceed through the Probation Service and the high levels of staffing required to manage these numbers.

Key figures: MoJ (2012) and NOMS (2013)

At the time of writing there are 35 Probation Trusts who have merged into one National Probation Service. In December 2012 the staffing ratio was:

- 16,524.88 full time staff employed and funded by the Probation Service (including Chief Executives);
- 4,408.31 Probation Service Officers made up the largest job group;
- 4,375.51 Probation Officer group and 3499.89 support staff/administration group;
- 14,662.47 staff working in an offender related function.

At the end of March 2013 the latest figures show:

- the Probation caseload was 222.306.

These figures are composed of:

- 112,090 offenders serving court orders comprising
    - 74,768 offenders being supervised under community orders
    - 37,865 offenders supervised under Suspended Sentence orders
- 111,511 offenders on the pre and post release caseload;
- added to this will be statutory supervision and rehabilitation to all 50,000 of those released following custodial sentences of 12 months and less;
- 42,793 court reports were prepared in the quarter ending June 2013;
- a community order can be imposed for up to the length of 3 years;
- it will contain at least 1 of the 12 requirements.

Functions of the Probation Service

Probation has a range of functions and it is important to give these functions careful consideration as they identify the different roles you would be required to undertake. These are outlined below:

- *Provide a service to the courts*: This would require you to do just that; you would be based in a court team and you would be the representative of the Probation Service and provide the court with information. This could be in the form of a general enquiry by the court officials or you may also take on the role of the probation prosecutor and present breach files in court.

- *Assessment and management of risk*: This function would begin following a request from the court. This would require you to make an assessment of both criminogenic and welfare needs and form the basis of a court report. Risk is assessed using a combination of actuarial risk assessment tools and clinical assessment skills. These risk assessments will inform strategies that contribute to effective risk management.

- *Preparation of pre-sentence reports to aid sentencing decisions*: The Crown and magistrates' courts will request a report and it is the function of the Probation Service to provide reports. As discussed above you would be required to prepare reports for the court whether you were court based or in a community team. These reports can take the form of a full pre-sentence report (PSR) or a fast delivery report (FDR). The report would include an assessment of not only the risk (of harm and re-offending) they pose but of the individual's circumstances and attitude to the offence.

*P*robation Service Officer, 'I was the court duty officer at our local magistrates' court. We do have a full time court duty officer; when he is unavailable on annual leave we go on a rota system to cover him. I conducted five oral reports that the bench requested and these were mainly to assess suitability for unpaid work and curfews.'

- *Supervise offenders on community orders, suspended sentences and licences*: This function is concerned with the rehabilitation of the offender. Once sentenced, the Probation Service would provide an end-to-end offender management. The assessment and management risk is central to the supervision plan. This would outline the intervention required to reduce the risk of re-offending and manage any

working in probation

risk of harm that may be present. The order/licence will be monitored accordingly and referral to relevant agencies for more specialist interventions would be made.

- *Provide a service to victims of crime*: This function requires probation staff to work with victims of violent or sexual crime where the offender has been sentenced to a year or more in prison. You may be based in a Victim Contact team, which means you will provide support to victims or their families through the Criminal Justice process and inform them of the offender's progress through their sentence. Probation staff also provides support for the restorative justice process and increase offenders' awareness of victims of their crimes.

*P*robation Service Officer, 'Meeting with the Victim Liaison Unit – As a victims champion for my probation office, I have to attend the VLUs monthly team meeting to report back any feedback from offender managers and also to inform OMs of any victims related changes. There was a presentation today by the Homicide Victim Support service, which I found very interesting.'

Working in the Probation Service

Joining the National Probation Service can provide an excellent career choice and the opportunity for career progression. Although the service is experiencing a period of change, both the National Probation Service and the National Offender Management Service recognise the need for experienced staff and will therefore continue to offer an excellent career structure. The service is made up of personnel carrying out a range of duties within different roles. These include Case Administrators, Unpaid Work Supervisors, Probation Service Officers, Programme facilitators, Assistants in Approved premises, Probation Officers, Hostel Managers, Senior Probation Officers, Area Managers, Assistant Chief Officers and then to Deputy or Chief Officers of Probation. So let us begin by considering the Probation Service Officer role.

Becoming a Probation Service Officer

Probation Service Officers carry out a wide range of duties. Some of these duties may appear to be similar to those of a Probation Officer but the interventions and assessment are with lower risk offenders. The Probation Service has a tiering system, which guides the management of offenders. This system is based on the risk of harm and the risk of re-offending that an offender has been assessed as posing. Not all offenders need to be managed by qualified Probation Officers and if assessed as a low risk offender they would be supervised by a Probation Service Officer to continue monitoring attendance, address specific needs through partnership agencies or supervision focussed on encouraging community integration.

Action point

When you are considering your career choices in the Probation Service you would benefit from completing some voluntary work experience in the Criminal Justice sector; although not essential it is desirable and would place you at an advantage when identifying and demonstrating skills and competencies.

---

*P*robation Service Officer, 'Volunteer first and get a flavour of what it is about.'

---

*A*ssessor and Trainer, 'Get more involved in community projects and try to get an all-round picture of court, prisons, probation etc. where you can.'

Entrance for unqualified staff into the National Probation Service is through the Probation Service Officer route. This includes those who are intending to complete the Probation Qualification Framework to become a qualified Probation Officer. Let us consider the options available.

Graduate and non graduate applicants – On joining the Probation Service you will be required to undertake training to enable you to practise. This would be in the form of a *Gateway to Practice induction programme*; some areas refer to this process as the *induction process* or the *introduction to practice*. It is covered over a 10 day period, but must be completed within 20 days of you joining the service. This induction will provide you with the basic understanding of the Service's key roles and functions. It will outline its expectations of you as an integral part of the Service and will also begin to help you to develop an understanding of the skills required to work effectively. These skills would include responding to diversity, communication skills, the assessment and management of risk and multi-agency and team work.

Non graduate – Once you have completed the induction you will be able to work with offenders and continue to develop your skills by taking *the Vocational Qualification Diploma in Probation Practice level 3 (VQ3)*. This must be undertaken within the first 12 month period of your employment and on completion you would be assessed as competent to practise as a Probation Service Officer. At this point in your career you may wish to consider your options, whether you wish to practise as a Probation Service Officer or develop your knowledge and skills in the Criminal Justice Sector further and complete a relevant degree on a part time basis.

Reflection point

It is important to note that until recently those Probation Service Officers who were already in a post and did not have a relevant degree could apply to the service to complete the

Probation Qualification Framework to become a Probation Officer. This enabled them to complete the Honours Degree in Community Justice and Vocational Qualifications Diploma in probation studies level 5 (VQ5). However, current changes in the Service may not see this pathway being available in the future.

Once you successfully complete the VQ3, you will be equipped with the skills to:

- assist in the assessment of risk of reoffending and harm
- value diversity
- communicate effectively
- support changes in behaviour
- work with others
- develop your own skills
- work within a specialist area.

Graduates – The entry route to become a Probation Officer is through the Probation Service Officer Graduate Diploma Pathway. If you have a relevant honours degree you are eligible to apply for the Probation Qualification Framework programme of study. The relevant honours degrees are identified by the National Offender Management Service and include: Police Studies, Criminology, Community Justice, Criminal Justice or a joint/combination degree that includes 50 per cent of these subject areas. There are discussions to expand the relevant degree but at the time of writing they stand. The relevant degree must not have been awarded more than five years ago.

*P*robation Service Officer, 'I wish I had known how important it was to understand the content of the degree I was going to study.'

Following a successful interview you would work as a Probation Service Officer and in some areas there is a further assessment centre selection process to place successful candidates on the graduate route. Once on the graduate route you would complete the *Vocational Qualification Diploma in Probation Practice level 5 (VQ5)* and the *Graduate Diploma*. Although guidelines differ from area to area, due to training and work-force planning needs, you would usually be in post for between 6–9 months and complete six of the twelve VQ5 Units before you commence on the academic component. The VQ5 is com-petency based and you are required to demonstrate your skills working with offenders. The academic component is currently provided by three universities, each with its own programme delivery. The curriculum is delivered in a blended learning style with a combination of face-to-face teaching at university work-shops, e-learning environments and written assignments. This route will take approximately 15 months to complete.

Reflection point

At the time of writing, the transforming rehabilitation agenda has not been clear in the training and qualifications it will require the Community Rehabilitation Companies to undertake.

Job description

The current changing landscape in the delivery of Probation Services will result in varying practices of advertising for the different posts. You must look for posts in both the Community Rehabilitation Companies and the National Probation Service. From my experience the Probation Service encourages applica-tions from a wide range of people, especially from mature applicants. This very rewarding yet challenging career path requires those who have some prior knowledge and experience in working with individuals from a wide range of backgrounds and life experiences. It is current practice for the employing area to advertise and recruit in the local areas, check out the areas you are interested in and familiarise yourself with their advertising and recruitment procedure. It is also important for you to have knowledge of the Community Rehabilitation Company to whom you may be applying.

As a Probation Service Officer you will be required to work 37 hours a week and as a guide the salary you could earn would be between £21,000 and £27,000 a year. Once qualified as a Probation Officer your starting salary could begin at £28,000 up to £35,000.

---

*P*robation Service Officer, 'Preparation – this is not a 9–5 job!'

Action point

For further information look on the following websites

Skills for Justice – www.sfjuk.com

Ministry of Justice – www.justice.gov.uk

Entry requirements

You must contact your local National Probation Service and/or the Community Rehabilitation Companies, as each area and the individual agency will stipulate the entry requirements. This would usually be:

- a good standard of education, GCSEs or equivalent;
- the potential and motivation to complete work-based qualifications (as above);

- some previous relevant experience of working with offenders or other vulnerable or excluded groups;
- if the application is to recruit potential Probation Officers via the Probation Service Officer Graduate route, you will need a relevant degree (as listed above).

The person specification will list both desirable (they prefer you to have it) and essential (they are required) qualities. These would need to be demonstrated in the application form and assessment process. These may include a combination of the following qualities:

- a demonstrated ability to work to deadlines and organise and prioritise work;
- good basic level qualifications;
- good oral communication;
- ability to work as part of a team;
- the commitment to undertake the relevant training and qualifications.

*H*uman Resources Officer, 'You will need to progress through the Disclosure and Barring Service. You would not be prevented from applying for this post if you have a criminal conviction as it is based on the conviction type and the length of time the offence occurred.'

Action point

Make a list of the requirements and qualities that you have.

Do they match this list?

Think about what you may need to do to develop your skills and match these qualities.

The application process

Vacancies for probation staff will be advertised in the local media and job agencies. You will be required to contact your local Service and request an *application pack*. This contains all the relevant information you will need to apply for the post. Please make sure you familiarise yourself with the documentation as this will provide a lot of the information needed to complete both your application form and more importantly your personal statement.

> **Action point**
>
> Look back at Chapter 4 for more information on completing the application form.

On successfully demonstrating you have met the essential and desirable entry criteria in your application form and personal statement, hopefully you will be offered the opportunity to attend the next stage; this is the Assessment Centre process.

Assessment Centre process

The Assessment Centre is not a place but a process. It has been developed to help areas select and recruit suitably skilled and experienced staff. The assessment is based on a combination of scores from different tasks and assessed by different assessors. This provides the opportunity to demonstrate your strengths in a range of tasks. The process will comprise a combination of the following exercises:

- a written exercise
- a group task
- a presentation
- a scripted interview
- a semi structured interview.

Action point

Look at the Internet for some examples of different assessment centre tasks and hints. I will begin by giving you two specific examples:

The *written exercise* would present you with a scenario and you would be required to reach a solution. The process of reaching the solution is the assessed piece of work. To demonstrate how you reached the solution you would need to include the following:

- *Introduction* – providing a brief overview of the scenario;
- *Solving the problem* – provide an explanation of what you are going to do;
- *Actions required* – demonstrate how you are going to achieve it;
- *Summary and conclusion* – present a brief overview of what you are suggesting and the reasons why.

When taking part in the *group exercise* you are being assessed on the following areas:

- an ability to relate to others;
- working as part of a team;
- your knowledge/understanding of group/individual work;
- communication;
- planning and organising;
- self-management (feedback);
- motivation and commitment;
- values;
- openness to new ideas;
- problem-solving skills.

Reflection point

At this point you would benefit from revisiting Chapter 4 and considering the Assessment Centre process in more depth.

Action point

List your skills and identify how you can demonstrate these skills to a potential employer.

A number of Probation Service Officers were asked to identify the three most important skills they use at work. Here are selections of their responses.

Probation Service Officer, 'Communication skills i.e. listening and negotiating; Organisation and flexibility because things change very quickly; Motivational interviewing.'

Probation Service Officer, 'Listening, multi-tasking, organisation.'

Probation Service Officer, 'Motivational skills, assessment skills, pro-social modelling.'

They were also asked what they wish they had known.

Probation Service Officer, 'It's the level of work and how this can impact on you physically and mentally. Never being able to clear my task list.'

O ne piece of advice they have for students.

Probation Service Officer, 'Get as much experience as you possibly can in the Criminal Justice field while at university because without it, you will find it extremely difficult to find employment in this sector. I think we are in an extremely lucky position in Criminal Justice because of the amount of volunteering opportunities there are within the statutory and non-statutory organisations, as well as charities.'

Action point

Having read the roles of the Probation Service Officer and the requirements of the Probation Qualification Framework consider the following:

- What attracts you to this career?
- What are your personal challenges for you in taking up this post?
- What is your motivation?
- What do you hope to achieve?

Working as a Probation Service Officer

Following success at interview and the Assessment Centre process you may be offered a position. We have discussed some of the further training and qualifications that you would complete to practise efficiently and also should you wish to follow the Probation Qualification Framework. This role would see you carrying out the functions of the National Probation Service or the Community Rehabilitation Companies and working directly with offenders in a range of capacities. You may be based in a court team and this would see you providing a service to the court by providing advice and guidance to the bench. You may prepare fast track reports or complete bail applications. Based in an Offender Management Unit you would be supervising lower risk offenders, carrying out the role of broker and supporting individuals to access services that will meet their needs. Working within the programmes team would require you to complete a training course, which would provide accreditation and following training you would become an accredited trainer delivering programmes to offender groups. See above for further information.

We approached some Probation Service Officers currently undertaking the Probation Qualification and asked them about the parts of the job they like. Here are some responses:

What they like:

- One-to-one interaction with our client group.
- Flexibility i.e. planning my own diary and the variety of the work.
- Excellent training/support to develop knowledge base and skills.
- Every day is different.
- Helping people.
- Seeing change.

What they are not so keen on:

- Report writing.
- Inefficiency of the organisation, i.e. I find the procedures very slow and it's difficult to change or challenge procedures to make them more effective.
- Lack of a 'social scene' within the organisation.
- Lots of computer work.
- Too much target driven work.
- Government bureaucracy.

Becoming a Probation Officer

Once you have successfully completed the Probation Qualifications Framework you will be qualified to work as a Probation Officer, however achieving your degree award does not automatically entitle you to a Probation Officer post. Many areas hold *competitive interviewing* for the vacancies they may have. Achieving the award would make you *eligible to apply* for a post within a chosen service, and the selection process would give you an opportunity to demonstrate the skills and knowledge you have acquired while completing your training. When vacancies arise, areas may use a variety of selection processes such as interviews and written exercises. These exercises will vary between services and areas but an example may be framed to assess your analytical and report writing skills.

Reflection point

Think about the personal attributes and professional skills listed below.

Personal attributes	*Professional skills*
mature and responsible attitude	good oral/written communication skills
ability to cope with stressful situations	professional relationship skills
integrity	team skills
open minded	ability to evaluate and assess
confident	motivation
committed	administration and computer skills
responsible	time keeping
respect for diversity	analytical

As a Probation Officer you will be required to assess and evaluate information. This will then inform your risk assessments and you will be expected to produce accurate reports for the courts, the parole boards and for the multi agency meetings. You will demonstrate an in-depth understanding of the social and personal factors that may underpin offending behaviour and use this knowledge to inform your interventions. Most importantly you will demonstrate your commitment to developing professional working relationships to aid the desistence process. You will monitor and record contacts and respond accordingly when there are unexplained absences. You will be accountable for public protection.

Action point

There are two very important skills that are essential to the Probation Officer role: reflection and building working relationships. Consider how you can demonstrate your understanding of these.

As part of our research for this chapter we approached some Probation Officers to give us an idea of their 'typical' working day:

Table 5.1 A Probation Officer's typical working day

Time and duration	Core activity – please describe the activity/task, what skills you may be using etc.	Activity category
9am	Supervision appointment Discussion regarding transfer of case as offender has moved	Face to face
9.25	Computer – read emails/reply Delius entry – email re case transferee	Admin Record keeping
9.45	Completed risk assessment for offender in prison regarding Cat D suitability	Risk assessment

10.00	Admin – Delius entries Breach letters x2	Admin
10.45	Started FDR (Fast Delivery report)	Report writing Court
12.00	Left office to travel to HMP Kirkham	Travel time
13.30	Prison visit	Face to face
15.00	Travel home	Travel time
16.30	Finish	

Becoming a Senior Probation Officer

Having developed your career in the National Probation Service as a Probation Officer you may wish to progress onto management level. You would be encouraged to consider your career options and taking on the role of Senior Probation Officer is a demanding and rewarding role. It is not uncommon for the areas to advertise senior positions in a temporary capacity to provide the opportunity for Probation Officers to 'Act up'. Working as an Acting Senior will give you the hands-on experience to help you understand the demands of the role. Some areas encourage Probation Officer grades to do a management qualification while in the role of a Probation Officer, other areas may support you in this process once appointed to the Senior Probation Officer role.

To be *eligible* to apply for a management position you must have work experience as a main grade practitioner. You will need to have the relevant qualifications, which include the Diploma in Probation Studies (DipSW), the Diploma in Social Work (DipSW), the Certificate and Qualification in Social Work (CQSW) or equivalent.

Areas will advertise their vacancies according to area policy; this would be in both the local and national newspapers as well as relevant websites. Areas differ in the recruitment process; usually it would include an application form and then a selection process, which may require you to complete a written task, deliver a presentation and attend for interview. But remember one of the essential qualities needed to manage a team is good leadership skills.

The Senior Probation Officer role varies depending on region and location; you may have responsibility for *managing more than one team* at different locations. Here are some of the responsibilities you may have:

Auditing and accountability – timeliness of court reports, maintaining service targets, auditing cases, quality assuring work, attending management meetings;

Managing staff – includes protecting and supporting staff, workload allocation, effective supervision, staff development, delivering team meetings, sharing information, managing sickness and absence;

Lead/organisational responsibilities – working with a wide range of partners at both strategic and operational level, such as taking the role of Chair of Multi Agency Public Protection Panels (MAPPPs), attending local initiatives such as Drug Action Teams, Community Groups, liaise with Social Services, encourage and engage with new innovations such as pilot projects.

Probation Service in Northern Ireland

Overview of the Probation Service in Northern Ireland

The Northern Ireland Probation Service is very similar to that of the English system. Practitioners are called Probation Service Officers and Probation Officers and the roles and functions are similar.

Action point

Revisit what you have read about the Northern Irish Criminal Justice System in Chapter 2 to help you understand how the Probation Service fits in with the wider system.

The Northern Irish Probation Service was in existence long before the Probation of Offenders Act 1907. This Act enabled magistrates to appoint Probation Officers to supervise defendants on a formal basis through a Probation Order. As with the rest of the Criminal Justice System the service has developed to respond to the growing needs of the wider Criminal Justice System. The modern day service is provided by the Probation Board Northern Ireland (PBNI), which came into effect in the early 1980s. This is a non-departmental public body and thus the board employs all probation staff and manages its own budget.

The Probation Board Northern Ireland have clearly identified their mission, aims and vision, and before you consider applying for a career with the service you need to have an understanding of these and consider how you can contribute to the overall work in the organisation.

Mission: to make the community safer through our work in managing offenders;

Aim: to reduce crime and the harm it does by challenging and changing offender behaviour;

Vision: to be an excellent organisation delivering best practice probation services and playing a central role in the management of offenders in Northern Ireland.

In order to achieve these goals the service is guided by a strong set of principles and a social work value base.

Reflection point

Take a look at the guiding values and principles – do you feel comfortable with them?

When we are carrying out our work:

- The knowledge, skills and commitment that our staff demonstrates is fundamental to success.

- We are committed to using research and evidence-based effective practice to inform all our work.
- We can be more effective when working in partnership with other departments, agencies, service providers and local communities.
- Respect for one another and the recognition and acknowledgement of the contribution of colleagues is essential.
- We value diversity and difference and treat people with respect.
- Everything we do will be underpinned by equality, openness, fairness, honesty and integrity.

Reflection point

It can be difficult to know what our value base may be but it is very important to understand that if you don't know your values and work with something that is against what you believe this will create stress.

Think about what you value and why you value it . . . continue asking questions so you can understand what it is you really do value.

Key facts (PBNI 2014)

- 13 board members sit on the Probation Board Northern Ireland;
- 400 + people are employed by the Probation Board Northern Ireland;
- half are Probation Officers who must hold a professional qualification;
- other staff include Probation Service Officers, managers, administration;
- 45 probation sites across Northern Ireland;
- PBNI also has a forensic psychology unit.
- Between 1 April–31 December 2013:
  - 7,674 court, parole and other assessment reports were prepared

- total caseload 4,552, of which 3,398 in the community and 1,154 in custody
  - 334 Combination Order
  - 785 Community Service Order
  - 144 Custody probation order
- 250,000 hours of unpaid work to the community were completed.

Becoming a Probation Officer in Northern Ireland

All Probation Officers must hold a *social work degree or a relevant qualification*. There are opportunities to work as support staff and these include Community Service Officers and Probation Service Officers. Working as a Probation Service Officer requires a commitment that you agree to undertake and achieve the Community Justice NVQ level 3 (VQ3) within two years of your appointment to the service. Should you wish to develop your career in the service and train to be a Probation Officer you would have to apply to do the Bachelor of Social Work course on a full time or part time basis.

Reflection point

Why do you need a social work qualification?

Due to the challenging nature of working with offenders who have experienced a range of social, personal and emotional problems you need to have a sound knowledge base of how problems impact on individuals in order to understand how best to intervene.

Action point

Queen's University offers three routes to the degree of Bachelor of social work.

- 64 places are available on a three-year programme;
- 40 places on a two-year course for students who already hold a relevant degree;
- 8 places on a five-year part-time route;
- application for all three routes is via UCAS.

University of Ulster offers:

- Three-year full time programme;
- Five-year part time programme;
- Two-year accelerated programme for those with a 2:2 in a relevant honours degree.

For further information go to Queens University at www.qub.ac.uk and University of Ulster at www.ulster.ac.uk.

Application and interview process

The Probation Board of Northern Ireland advertise their vacancies on their recruitment website and in the local and regional media, so it is advisable to note what days the media hold the job advertisements and check regularly.

Eligibility

Vacancies are open to UK nationals, Commonwealth Citizens, British Protected Persons and European Economic Area (EEA) national, Swiss nationals or a person who is not an EEA or Swiss national, but is a family member of a UK or Irish national, or is a family member of an EEA national who has moved to the UK from another EEA member state for an approved purpose.

Application packs are available on request and can be downloaded from the PBNI website. Please make sure you read all of the relevant literature as the pack contains the job description, person specification and vetting information. It is your responsibility to complete your application in the time permitted and make sure it details how you match the criteria.

If you are successful you will be called for interview. Interviews are based on the *competencies* required to fulfil the advertised role. These competencies are a combination of knowledge, skills, motivations and personal traits. The scoring mechanism is based on a seven point scale from one (weakness) to seven (exceptionally strong). If you are successful in achieving a score that makes you employable, you may be successful in being offered a post. Those who meet the criteria can be placed on a waiting list and offered vacancies for up to 12 months after interview. Being offered a post is dependent on successful pre-employment checks that have been made.

Currently all candidates are vetted under the Counter Terrorism Check (CTC) and Access NI enhanced level.

The Probation Service in Scotland

Overview of the Scottish Probation System

Developing your career in the Criminal Justice field in Scotland provides a similar framework for practice but Probation Officers are Criminal Justice social workers. Having read Chapter 2 you will have some understanding of some of the differences in the Criminal Justice System in Scotland from those in Northern Ireland, England and Wales. Although a Probation Service was initially established in 1905, around the same time as the service in England, the Probation Service was disbanded as a national body in 1968 and integrated into generic social work departments, through the Social Work (Scotland) Act 1968. It is important to be aware that the Scottish Criminal Justice System, as with the rest of the United Kingdom Criminal Justice System, is experiencing rapid change and you would benefit from making yourself familiar with these changes.

Reflection point

Although the Probation services in England and Scotland were implemented around the same time they had different origins. The Scottish system was not based on missionary ideals but focussed on the American initiative, the service to the court was provided by plain clothes Police Officers and was initially developed as a response to a concern with the high numbers of inmates in the Prison System. This concern continues to inform the Scottish Criminal Justice practices today.

Action point

Familiarising yourself with the history of the Scottish Probation System and the Criminal Justice social work model will help you to understand the role of the service in Scotland and give you insight into the development of the services social work values. Reading McIvor and McNeill (2007) will give you a broad understanding of the changes in the system.

When considering a career in the Criminal Justice Service it is also important to familiarise yourself with the aims, objectives and responsibilities of the system you are considering applying to, as meeting and fulfilling these aims and objectives will be linked to the assessment criteria.

The key objective of the Criminal Justice Services is to:

- achieve a reduction in re-offending;
- increase social inclusion of former offenders; and
- support victims of crime.

Criminal Justice Social Work Services main aims include:

- tackling criminal behaviour and reducing the risk of re-offending;
- supervising offenders in the community;
- assisting prisoners to re-settle into the community after release from custody.

Understanding how these aims and objectives will be met by the potential employers is essential knowledge when weighing up whether or not this is the chosen career for you. Understanding the functions will also equip you with baseline knowledge for preparing for interview as the potential employers will be looking for your understanding and commitment to carrying out the functions. The main functions of Criminal Justice social workers include:

- the assessment and preparation of reports on offenders to assist the courts decisions on sentencing;
- court social work services to assist those attending court whether as witnesses, accused people or offenders;
- bail information and supervision services as an alternative to custodial remand;
- supervising offenders in the community on community payback/probation orders to tackle offending behaviour;
- supervising offenders on drug treatment and testing orders to reduce drug related crime;
- supervising offenders on unpaid work/community service orders who are required to perform unpaid, useful work for the benefit of the community;
- prison social work services to prisoners and their families;
- preparing reports for the Parole Board to assist decisions about release from prison;

- through care services including parole, supervised release and other prison aftercare orders to assist public safety and community protection;
- supporting victims of crime and their families.

Key figures (Audit Scotland (2011) and Scottish government (2012))

- There are 8 Community Justice Authorities responsible for 32 local authorities.
- The 32 local authorities now have responsible for the planning and delivery of local services.
- Criminal Justice social workers are employed by the local authority.
- Probation Services are reserved for those over the age of 16.
- The average cost of providing a social enquiry report varies between £270 and £565.
- The average cost of implementing a probation order ranges from £1,013–£1,790.
- The average cost of a community service order ranges from £1,838–£3,116.
- 36,367 Criminal Justice reports have been prepared.
- 19,746 total orders commenced of which:

  - 3,040 Probation Orders
  - 2,877 supervised attendance orders
  - 557 drug treatment and testing orders
  - 10,228 community payback order.

- For those offences committed after February 2011 the community payback order has replaced the Community Service Orders, Probation Orders and supervised attendance orders.
- The community payback order has nine requirements. The courts can impose one or more of these requirements.

working in probation

Action point

The Scottish Social work Council (SSSC) has published the Codes of Practice for Social Workers and employers, which set out the standards of practice expected in day-to-day working. Access and read these codes.

Becoming a Criminal Justice worker and Criminal Justice social worker in Scotland

The minimum qualification needed to become a Criminal Justice social worker is an Honours Degree in social work. For those graduates who have completed a BA Honours degree you may wish to consider completing a postgraduate degree in social work. These qualifications can be gained from a range of different universities across Scotland and both the Open University and the Robert Gordon University (Aberdeen) offer these courses on a distance learning basis.

If you are serious about following this career route you must discuss your options with your careers advisor as courses may alter or be removed or added depending on workforce demands. There are several options for you to consider:

- You could begin by taking an *HNC* in social care. You would need at least 120 hours' practice experience, and this could be voluntary or paid work, and you need two Highers (Higher is one of the national school-leaving certificate exams offered by the Scottish Qualifications authority). One needs to preferably be in English.
- This would then lead the entry range of a HND in social science.
- This would make you eligible to apply for second year (or third year) of some relevant social science degrees.

Action point

There are a range of degree and postgraduate courses on offer by higher educational institutes – these are full and part time courses that take between three and five years to complete.

For further information take a look at these websites:

Robert Gordon University www.rgu.ac.uk
Open University www.open.ac.uk

Remember to consider the level of commitment required as you would need to complete a six months working placement and have to self-fund at a cost of approximately £3,090 per year.

You can also begin your career without any formal qualifications, you may decide the time is not right for you or you do not meet the entry requirements for training in social work, or you may not be in a position to take the qualification at this moment in time – then there are a range of other options available to you. You could begin by applying for a post as an unqualified Criminal Justice Officer. But you must be willing to complete qualifications while in this post. This route would enable you to develop the knowledge and skills of working in the Criminal Justice System and you would be able to complete the Scottish Vocational Qualifications (SVQs). These are work-based assessments that assess knowledge, skills and values in relation to a range of job roles. Newly qualified social workers in Scotland earn around £25,000 rising to between £29,000 and £35,000 a year with experience. Practice team leaders earn from £37,000 a year. Directors in local authorities can earn over £100,000 a year.

Application process

- Criminal Justice Workers and Criminal Justice social workers are employed by the Local Authority.

- Posts will be advertised in the Local authority, national media and through registered agencies.
- You will be required to request and complete an application form.
- Your route into social work would be either via the BA Honours social work degree or the post graduate social work qualification (or other recognised equivalent i.e. CQSW, Dip SW, CCETSW).
- You must be registered with the Scottish Social Services.
- This must demonstrate the key skills as identified in the job description and person specification.
- Successful applicants are invited for interview.

 Applicants will be vetted through the *Protecting Vulnerable Groups Scheme.*

Reflection point

The role of the Criminal Justice worker is similar to that of the Probation Service Officer in England and Wales and you would benefit from reading that section in this chapter.

Chapter summary

This chapter has considered the Probation Systems in England, Wales, Northern Ireland and Scotland. It has explored the different roles available within the service and provided information on the entry criteria, recruitment process and the career progression opportunities available. There are action and reflection points for you to think about and possibly link your skills to that of the organisation you may be considering applying to. We hope you enjoyed the top tips from the practitioners in the field.

Top tips

- Think of your contribution to a team.
- How do you know you have communicated effectively?
- How do you make your degree relevant?
- What is the core focus of your dissertation/work-based Learning Project?
- How can you evidence your skills?
- Understand the organisation.
- Take time to read and familiarise yourself with the recruitment process.
- Give yourself time to complete the application form correctly.
- Practise your communication skills.
- Understand the assessment criteria.
- Know the difference between essential and desirable selection criteria.
- Practise your presentation skills, including your non-verbal communication.
- Be aware of your values and motivations.
- Think about why you want the job that you have applied for.

Recommended reading

History of the UK Services

McIvor, G. and McNeill, F. (2007) Probation in Scotland: Past, present and future. In L. Gelsthorpe and R. Morgan (Eds). *Handbook of Probation* (pp. 131–154). Devon: Willan Publishing

Mair, G. and Burke, L. (2011) *Redemption, Rehabilitation and Risk Management: A history of probation.* Oxon: Routledge

Making the Difference: An Oral History of Probation in Northern Ireland at its Centenary and in the 25th Year of the Probation Board for Northern Ireland. Compiled by: Brendan Fulton; Edited by: Trevor Parkhill. Retreived from www.pbni.org.uk/archive/Guide%20to%20Information/The%20services%20we%20offer/Leaflets%20bktls%20newsletters/pbni%2025th%20book.pdf (accessed 27 May 2014)

O'Mahony, D. and Chapman, T. (2007) Probation, the state and community – delivering probation services in Northern Ireland. In L. Gelsthorpe and R. Morgan (Eds). *Handbook of Probation* (pp. 155–178). Devon: Willan Publishing

Guide to practice

Canton, R. (2011) *Probation Working with Offenders*. Oxon: Routledge

Pycroft, A. and Gough, D. (Eds) (2010) *Multi-agency Working in Criminal Justice*. Bristol: Policy Press

Robinson, A. (2011) *Foundations for Offender Management*. Bristol: Policy Press

Web sources

- www.skillsdevelopmentscotland.co.uk – Scotland development site
- www.pbni.org.uk is the Probation board of Northern Ireland website. This site will provide extensive and detailed information about the service you may be wishing to join

References

Audit Scotland (2011) An overview of the Scottish Criminal Justice System. Retrieved from www.audit-scotland.gov.uk/docs/central/2011/nr_110906_justice_overview.pdf (accessed 27 May 2014)

Home Office (2004) Bold Steps – National Probation Service for England and Wales 2004–2005 Business Plan [Electronic Version]. London: HMSO

Ministry of Justice (n.d) Probation Service Workforce Information Summary Report: Quarter 3 2012/13. Retrieved from the Ministry of Justice website: www.gov.uk/government/uploads/system/uploads/attachment_data/file/218379/probation-workforce-report-q3–2012–13-staff.pdf (accessed 27 May 2014)

Ministry of Justice (n.d.) Offender Management Statistics April–June 2013. Retrieved from www.gov.uk/government/uploads/system/uploads/attachment_data/file/253986/omsq-bulletin-apr-june-2013.pdf (accessed 27 May 2014)

National Offender Management Service (2013) Commissioning Intentions from 2014. Retrieved from www.justice.gov.uk/downloads/about/noms/commissioning-intentions-2014.pdf (accessed 27 May 2014)

National Probation Directorate (2001) A New Choreography. An integrated strategy for the National Probation Service for England and Wales. London: National Probation Directorate

Probation Board Northern Ireland (n.d) Caseload Statistics Quarter 3, 2013–2014. Retrieved from PBNI website www.pbni.org.uk/archive/pdfs/About%20Us/Statistics%20and%20Research/Caseload%20Statistics/Caseload%20Trends%20Report%2031%20December%202013%20Internet.pdf (accessed 27 May 2014)

Scottish Government Publications (2012) Criminal Justice social work statistics, 2011–2012. Retrieved from the Scottish government website www.scotland.gov.uk/Publications/2012/12/1332 (accessed 27 May 2014)

Working in the Police

Introduction to the Police Service

The Police, as part of the Criminal Justice System, focus on maintaining law and order. The main functions of the Police are identified as being: the promotion of safety, the reduction of disorder, the reduction of crime, the reduction of the fear of crime, the investigation of crime and the delivery of justice. Working within the modern Police Service will require you to be adaptable, resilient, patient, respectful, a good team member, a good decision maker and a good communicator. As with many other sectors of the Criminal Justice Service, the Police Service has a commitment to working in a multi-disciplinary way with those with whom it serves and essentially the community plays a key role in the operation and management of the Police. The Crime and Disorder Act 1998 provides the legal framework from which the Police need to adopt a multi-disciplinary approach to their work and engage within a framework of community policing.

Reflection point

Take time to have a look at The Crime and Disorder Act 1998. Note down the agencies that the Police have a duty to engage with in relation to crime and disorder reduction. Have a think also about what this may mean in practice for the organisations involved and the work of the Police.

It is crucial when considering a career in the Police that you consider the factors that have been influential in the directions that the Police Service has taken and the people that it works with, and how this may impact on the role you will have. At the time of writing the College of Policing is pioneering a three year programme aimed at trying to establish an 'evidence' base for the Police Service across most services, but especially in England and Wales to assist them in tackling local crime, while at the same time managing this with a reduced number of staff. Take time to have a look at the College of Policing website, as more detailed information is contained along with other useful resources. You would also benefit from reading more in depth texts and refer to The Policing Matters series.

Action point

Review Chapter 2 of this book and note down some of the key points raised about the Police and policing, and think about their implications for you working in this sector of the Criminal Justice System.

Having reviewed Chapter 2 of this book you will have an understanding of the role of the Police Service in the Criminal Justice System. This chapter will build on this knowledge by providing the reader with a *brief overview* of the Police, its development and its current position within the Criminal Justice System. Importantly, within this, the organisation, governance and role of the Police Service will be discussed and the key debates highlighted. *Key figures* will be presented throughout the chapter in relation to the organisation of the Police, the numbers of people working within the Police and the predicted future employment trends. The chapter will then move on to consider the range of roles and careers available within the Police Service and, in doing so, the competencies, skills and values required to work in this sector will be discussed.

The Police Service offers a wide range of different career options as well as a range of opportunities for career enhancement/development. Skills for Justice (2009) have highlighted that around 50 per cent of the overall workforce of the Criminal Justice sector in the UK are employed in the Police. Within this chapter the roles discussed will be those of a *Police Officer*, *Police Community Support Officers* and *special constables*. We have selected these specific roles/careers as they provide the reader with insight into the work that the Police do and the natural career progression through the service, and also due to the feedback received from students currently studying on related degree programmes. The entry requirements and application process will be considered for each role before moving through to a more general analysis of the skills needed to be successful in securing employment within this part of the Criminal Justice System.

It is important to note here that while in 2010 a number of different forces across the UK suspended their recruitment processes as a result of cuts to funding, these are now back in operation with forces advertising posts as they become available. In relation to this, some areas are considering the way that recruitment as a special can lead to entry to becoming a Police Officer and how this may be supported by programmes of study available in either universities or further education establishments.

It is this chapter's intention to provide the *practical advice and guidance* you will need to assist you in beginning to develop an awareness of what working within the Police Service will be like, what career opportunities are available, what skills and knowledge you will need to be able to carry out the role and hopefully dispel any myths that you may have.

Within the chapter there will be a separate discussion about the recruitment processes and practice in England and Wales, Scotland and Northern Ireland. Again it is important that you consider these differences and the implications of them for the area and role that you wish to work in.

Throughout the chapter you will recognise similarities between the practice and processes of recruitment in England and Wales, Scotland and Northern Ireland. The linked action points, reflection points and comments from those working in the sector are therefore important for you to consider in their entirety.

Action point

Have a look at the different Police Service websites for England and Wales, Scotland and Northern Ireland and write down the different roles that are available. What are the differences between the areas and the work that you would be required to be involved in?

Brief general overview of the Police Service

The primary aim of the Police is to work towards making communities safer by ensuring that the law is upheld, with those who break the law being brought to justice. The policing mission clearly states:

> I do solemnly and sincerely declare and affirm that I will well and truly serve the Queen in the office of constable, with fairness, integrity, diligence and impartiality, upholding fundamental human rights and according equal respect to all people; and that I will, to the best of my power, cause the

peace to be kept and preserved and prevent all offences against people and property; and that while I continue to hold the said office I will, to the best of my skill and knowledge, discharge all the duties thereof faithfully according to the law.

(Police Act 1996, Schedule 4)

The development of the modern Police Service in the UK can be traced back to Robert Peel through the Metropolitan Police Act 1829. The objective and vision at the time was to establish an organisation that would work to maintain order and control by detecting and preventing crime. The practice of the Police became standardised and answerable to the public. As part of this development the 'Peelian Principles' as they became known were established (Wright 2002).

The British model of policing that developed as a result of these principles saw the Police as citizens in uniform that exercised their powers by consent. For the Police this means that the majority of society allows them to fulfil their role.

Action point

Locate and consider the nine principles as described by Robert Peel. What do you think are the implications of these principles for modern day policing?

These principles have been developed throughout the last two centuries in relation to crime-orientated policing, community policing and in relation to the control and maintenance of order.

*P*olice Officer, 'What the Police do and should do is a constant cause for debate. There are so many different competing targets to be met. Sometimes it is an impossible task to get right.'

The structure of policing in England and Wales

Within England and Wales at the time of writing there are currently 43 different geographic forces. All of these forces have a designated structure and are 'led' by a Chief Constable. These 43 areas are responsible to The Home Office and, in addition to this, specialist Police forces exist such as the British Transport Police. Within these 43 areas, at the time of writing, around 140,000 Police Officers, 18,000 Special Constables and 15,800 Community Support Officers are employed by the Police Service in England and Wales (Prospects, January 2014).

The Home Office regulates the pay, conditions of service and the discipline of the Police Services. The Home Office are clear in stating that it is important that they work in partnership with the local areas and the community to set priority targets for the work that the Police do.

Action point

Have a look at the Home Office website. How could the work that you would do in the Police contribute to the reduction of crime?

Reflection point

Thames Valley Police Area for example state clearly on their website that their values relate to treating everyone with respect: engaging, listening, responding and acting on behalf of the community that it serves.

It is important to think about your own value base and link this to the area that you want to work in.

Every appointed officer in England and Wales is known as a 'constable' and it is from the Office of Constable that the Police receive the powers that they have. Regardless of educational background, all newly appointed Police Officers will start at this position and will have progressed through the different ranks available.

Within the Police in England and Wales there is a clearly defined rank structure and with the exception of the two London forces, The Metropolitan Police and the City of London Police, the chief officers are known as Chief Constables. In the Metropolitan Police and the City of London Police they are known as Commissioners. Chief Constables and Commissioners hold the responsibility for appointing, promoting and managing all Police Officers below the rank of Assistant Chief Constable.

Please see flow chart below.

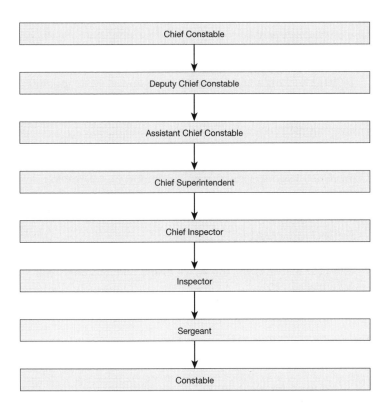

Figure 6.1 Ranks of Police in England and Wales

Reflection point

Take time to reflect on the rank structure of the Police and the different roles available. Think about how you may 'fit' into this rank structure.

The Police Service is a constantly evolving organisation and since the Royal Commission on Police in 1962 a number of different reforms have been passed by parliament. This piece of legislation, however, encapsulated the concept that policing should be governed by the people that they serve and by consent. The Police Reform Act 2002 extended the way in which other 'civilian' members of society could use the powers of the Police. These include Community Support Officers, a role to be discussed later in this chapter, detention officers and escort officers.

In 2012 41 Police and Crime Commissioners were appointed in England and Wales. The intended aim of the Police Crime Commissioners is to work within their local area/community to ensure that the needs of the local communities are being met and that the Police are held to account for their decisions and actions. There has been much debate about the effectiveness of Police Crime Commissioners and this will be important for you to think about.

Reflection point

The next elections for the Police Crime Commissioners will take place in 2016.

Becoming a Police Officer in England and Wales

The Police Service, regardless of area, encourages applicants from a range of different backgrounds. The Police Service encourages applications from a wide range of age groups and welcomes applications from people wishing to look for a career change.

The role of a Police Officer is both demanding and diverse. Police Officers work in a variety of different capacities but all work in partnership with their local communities and other parts of the Criminal Justice sector to assist in reducing crime and protecting the public. As a Police Officer, a variety of different and specialist roles are available and these are all available to those who have completed their period of 'probation'.

*P*olice Officer, 'It is important that you take time to research and reflect on the different roles available and think about how the work that you will be required to do is suited to your own skills, values and motivators. How policing is delivered in practice also depends upon the community it serves.

It is important to understand your values and be self-aware.'

Action point

Have a look at the Police Service website for the area you are interested in applying for and do the following:

* note down its local priorities;
* note down its organisational structure;
* note down the different roles available.

As a Police Officer starting your career you will likely be involved in a range of different activities that may include: working with different community groups; patrolling communities on foot, car or even bicycle; responding to calls; dealing with sensitive issues; interviewing suspects, victims and witnesses; preparing crime reports; presenting case files; giving evidence in court and investigating information received from members of the public.

Within each of these activities people will look to you for guidance and protection, so it is essential that you ensure that you have the skills needed to fulfil these roles.

Reflection point

Reflect on the different activities that the Police are required to be involved in.

What skills do you have that would enable you to fulfil these roles?

What skills will you need to develop?

It is important that you think about these different activities and skills, as they will be essential in the recruitment process. By taking the time to read this chapter and researching the role further you will greatly increase your chances of successfully becoming a Police Officer.

Key competencies needed to become a Police Officer in England and Wales

In 2011 a new Policing Professional Framework was launched as a result of a partnership between Skills for Justice and The National Policing Improvement Agency. This integrated competency framework provides ranks profiles, level profiles and skill requirements that the Police will have to work to.

Action point

Have a look at the Skills for Justice website. Locate the national role descriptors for a constable. Write down the personal qualities and skills that are listed and think about how you could demonstrate these in the recruitment process.

Below are listed some of the competencies that you will need to demonstrate (please look at Skills for Justice website for the full list of competencies):

Openness to change: This competency requires you to be adaptable to the work that you do.

Ability to communicate effectively: This competency relates to your ability to be clear and precise in the way that you communicate different types of information to different audiences. It is identified as one of the key skills required, as Police Officers communicate with a variety of people in a range of different settings.

> *P**olice Officer*, 'You have to really want to be a Police Officer as the challenges that you face in your day-to-day work can be daunting. Being able to get along with people and communicate is an essential skill and one which really does make the job easier.'

Ability to have a community and customer focus: This competency requires you to be able to build positive relationships with the community you serve and to be able to view situations from a range of perspectives. It is vital that as a Police Officer you are able to understand what the public wants/needs and how best to respond or not.

Ability to take ownership of your personal responsibility: This competency requires you to act responsibly and to be able to deal with any issues that you may face. It is important that as a Police Officer you are accountable for your actions on an individual level and on an organisational level.

Ability to be resilient: This competency requires you to respond logically and confidently despite the situations that you may encounter.

Ability to problem solve: This competency requires you to have the ability to look at situations from a variety of different sources and identify the most appropriate course of action.

This is a crucial aspect of the work that the Police do, as you will be faced with situations where you are required to manage a process that leads to the resolution of a 'problem'.

Ability to respect diversity: This competency requires you to be able to treat all people with dignity and respect despite their race, gender, age, sexuality, religion, class, ability/disability, language or appearance and to try to adopt a range of perspectives.

Ability to work within a team: This competency requires you to work as part of a team in all areas of your work to ensure the successful completion of tasks etc. You will also be required to demonstrate your ability to develop positive working relationships within the team.

Action point

Take time to think about the above competencies. Within each of the competencies identify the indicators that you will be assessed against. In relation to the competencies think of and note down an example that you could demonstrate for each. It is important to consider what the competencies would require of you if you were a Police Officer.

As a Police Officer working in England and Wales you will receive a wide range of benefits, flexible working hours, paid overtime as appropriate and around 23 days leave. The starting salary at the time of writing is around £23,000 and this salary is incremental, rising with each year of experience. Dependent upon your position you can expect your salary to increase to around £41,000 for a sergeant and £50,000 for an inspector. Within the Police there is a clearly defined promotional structure and you will be supported internally with these applications. As a Police Officer you will usually work a 40-hour week. This will be organised in different shift patterns.

Eligibility requirements

Within this section the more general entry requirements will be discussed but it is important that you also consider any local differences that may apply to the area that you are applying for. As previously stated the Police service, regardless of area, encourages applicants from a range of different backgrounds, experiences and age groups.

To be considered for the role of a Police Officer, however, you will need:

- to be between 18–60 (normal retirement age);
- to be either a British citizen, a citizen of the EU, or a commonwealth citizen or a foreign national with granted permissions to remain indefinitely within the UK;
- to have been resident in the UK for a minimum of three years;
- to declare any criminal convictions (you may still be eligible if you have minor convictions or cautions) in relation to this point you are advised to seek advice and clarification from the Police Service you are applying to;
- to be physically and mentally able to engage in Police duties;
- to meet minimum eyesight standards.

In addition to the above criteria you will be required to undergo a series of different assessments and tests and these will be discussed later in the chapter. It is important that you consider your eligibility fully before you take time to apply. You should also take time to consider the area that you want to apply for as applications can only be made to one area at a time. There are no minimum educational criteria set in place but it is important that you are aware that you will be required to undertake both written and numerical tests during the recruitment and selection process.

If you consider yourself to be eligible you will need to apply directly to the local area in which you want to work and for any vacancies that there may be.

Action point

The police.uk website has a full directory available of the UK Police forces. Investing some time in understanding the requirements of the different areas will assist you in the recruitment process for the area that you finally apply to.

There are various stages to the application process and these will now be discussed.

The application process

Police Officer jobs as with many other jobs in the sector are advertised in a range of different places. A useful starting point would be the local media and the Internet site for the Police Service you wish to apply to. It is important that you keep yourself up-to-date with the opportunities that are available and check these regularly.

> **P**olice Officer, 'It is important that you check the vacancies section of the area that you want to work in regularly as vacancies can be available for time limited periods.'

Within the application process there are a number of different stages. This may vary from area to area. You will need to pass each stage of the application process to be eligible to continue.

Stage 1:

This stage is usually *completed online* following a registration process. During this stage you will be required to complete an *eligibility assessment*. You may also be required to complete a *questionnaire* that looks at your suitability for the role of a Police Officer. It is likely that this questionnaire will be competency based and at the end of the test you will have an option as to whether you continue or not.

In some areas two further tests are taken during this stage, and these are also *competency based* and look at your attitude towards a set of statements and how you would respond to situations that you may face as a Police Officer.

If you are successful at this stage you will be invited to complete Stage 2 of the process.

Stage 2:

The main focus at this stage of the process is the completion of an *application form*. Again you need to be successful at this stage to progress to the next stage of the process. *What is crucial here is that you read the requirements of the application form fully and you complete all sections.* Take time to complete the application form and check your work fully for punctuation, grammatical and spelling errors.

Action point

The Police place a great deal of importance on a candidate's ability to use the English language correctly as discussed above. To improve the skills that you may have in this area, try to read a range of different literature sources. Read also the rules of grammar and practise your spelling.

Stage 3:

This stage of the process requires you to take part in an *assessment centre day*. This part of the process is concerned with testing your potential to perform the role of a Police Officer effectively. The standards to be met are set by the National College of Policing. During the assessment centre day you will be required to take part in a series of *role play* scenarios, a *competency based interview*, a *verbal and numeracy test* and two *written* exercises. These activities are all designed with the Police core competencies in mind. Throughout the assessment centre day you will be required to evidence a range of skills and the purpose of all the activities is to determine how you would respond to situations you might have to face in practice. Each different activity will be fully explained in advance and you will also be sent the relevant information needed prior to attending.

Reflection point

Think back to competencies discussed in Chapter 4 of this text. You may also want to refer to other chapters where competency based assessments are discussed. How could you evidence these competencies in a verbal and written form?

*C*areers Advisor, 'Evidence from students' participation in similar tests as part of an employability related module has shown that Criminal Justice students rate below the national graduate average for their maths ability. Practice makes perfect especially in relation to maths. GCSE Bitesize maths is a good resource to use.'

Action point

Take time to look at the following websites: policeuk.com and college.police.uk. Both of these websites contain detailed information regarding the activities required of you on the day and provide practice examples for you to complete.

It is important that you take time to prepare for the activities that you will have to take part in.

*P*olice Officer, 'The interview part of the day was so nerve racking. I wished that I had focussed more on the skills and competencies.'

Action point

Review the STAR method discussed in Chapter 4. Prepare answers to evidence the above skills and write these down.

Think about what the purpose of the written paper is.

Remember the importance of getting your grammar, spelling and punctuation correct.

Stages 4 and 5:

These stages are concerned with a medical and fitness assessment and references and security checks.

If you are successful in *ALL* elements of the recruitment process you will be formally appointed and offered a start date for the Police Training Course that you will need to complete before commencing employment.

Please note that in some areas you will also be required to complete the Certificate in Knowledge of Policing prior to commencing the training. Further information about the course can be found on the College of Policing website. There is a cost for the course of around £1,000, although this may vary depending on who is delivering the course, and you will need to be committed to both taught and self-study sessions of around 300 hours in total. Once completed the course is valid for three years.

Reflection point

Think about the commitment to study both in relation to the time commitment but also in relation to the cost.

What happens once I am appointed?

Once you are appointed you will spend your first two years on a period of 'probation'. The Initial Police Learning and Development Programmes (IPLDP) is an integral part of your first two years. This programme is a level 3 qualification and leads to a Diploma in Policing.

While local areas take responsibility for the delivery of the programme, the programme will be organised in four distinct training phases. These phases will focus on increasing your knowledge of the organisation, health and safety, human rights, community engagement, race and diversity and ICT. An integral component of the phases will be focussed on you engaging in work-based learning activities that combine operation duties with simulated incidents that you may have to deal with.

Within each of these phases the activities will be a combination of class-based and distance learning and independent patrol. You will be assessed throughout and will be required at the end of the training to submit a portfolio of evidence. This will be based on your ability to demonstrate how you would perform policing tasks and how you would demonstrate the personal qualities of a Police Officer.

Again it is important that you look at the individual force websites for specific details of the training requirements.

All Police areas pride themselves in the on-going professional development opportunities and training, and support is an integral part of this.

Once you have completed the two year 'probation' period you are eligible to apply to work in the range of specialist units that the Police have and be given the opportunity to take qualifying exams that lead to promotion through the rank structure.

Becoming a Police Leader in England and Wales

Within the Police there are many opportunities for career progression both within the variety of roles available but also in relation to you being promoted through the rank structure as stated.

The skills that need to be evidenced throughout this process are:

* leadership
* decision-making
* management skills
* managing budgets
* accountability
* adaptability
* responding to challenges
* responding to uncertain environments.

The Police High Potential Development Scheme

This scheme is designed to assist the Police in developing its future leaders. The programme lasts for five years and takes place in three phases. Throughout the programme there is a combined focus on skills development, academic learning and operational practice. This programme is delivered in partnership with Warwick Business School.

There are different stages to the application process and you will be required to complete a formal application form, written exercises, a situational judgement test and an assessment centre exercise.

Assessment Centres can be either a process or an actual event. The exercises are designed to see how you would respond to situations that you may have to deal with in your day-to-day job. There are a number of different website resources that provide guidance to assist you in developing these skills.

Graduate entry programmes

There are a number of different graduate entry programmes in England and Wales. It is important to look at the individual force websites for specific recruitment details. It is also, at this point, worth considering the graduate level opportunities available in other organisations such as MI5. This will be discussed in more detail in Chapter 10 of this book.

Becoming a Police Community Support Officer in England and Wales

Police Community Support Officers (PCSO) were introduced in 2002 under the Police Reform Act 2002 as a direct consequence of increases in demand and the challenges faced by those working in policing. Within the work of the Police, Community Support Officers are now firmly established and hold an important and integral role.

Police Community Support Officers fulfil a unique role within the Police that focuses on providing a visible presence and on tackling anti-social behaviour and environmental and fear of crime issues. As a Police Community Support Officer you would be required to work along with the Police in a specific targeted area and support them in their duties.

Each local Police area sets their own specific entry requirements and roles for the Police Community Support Officers
so it is important that you check this out.

In general, to apply for a position as a Police Community
Support Officer you do not need any formal qualifications. The
focus throughout the application stage is on your skills, attitude,
character and personal qualities.

Skills and attributes identified as being essential:

- confident
- experience in dealing with and managing difficult situations
- be sensitive
- communication skills
- team working
- patience.

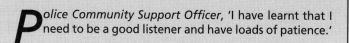

*P*olice Community Support Officer, 'I have learnt that I
need to be a good listener and have loads of patience.'

Day-to-day duties however could include:

- visibility patrol
- tackling anti-social behaviour
- gathering criminal intelligence
- dealing with minor offences
- crime prevention activities.

The powers that you would have working as a Police
Community Support Officer would vary depending upon where

you work. You would *not* have the same powers as a Police Officer and so you *do not have the powers to arrest, interview or process people.* Standard powers were, however, introduced for all Police Community Support Officers in 2007 regardless of the area worked in.

The powers of a Police Community Support Officer:

- the power to issue fixed penalty notices;
- the power to confiscate alcohol and tobacco;
- the power to obtain the personal details of anyone acting in an anti-social way;
- the power to enter a premises if it is to save or protect life or to prevent any damage being caused;
- the power to remove any abandoned vehicles.

As a Police Community Support Officer you would be required to work a shift pattern that includes weekends and bank holidays. It is important to consider that most of your working day will be spent outside: patrolling the streets, giving talks and building relationships with the local community. Starting salaries vary but will be in the region of £18,000.

Reflection point

Consider the implications this may have on your lifestyle. Would this suit you?

The recruitment process

In general to apply to become a Police Community Support Officer you do not need to hold any formal qualifications but you will be required to pass a fitness and medical test.

The recruitment and selection process for Police Community Support Officers varies between different Police forces so it is important that you take time to look at the information provided by the area that you want to work for. *This is also important because you are only entitled to apply to one area/force at a time.* However, in general, in England and Wales the recruitment process would require you to complete an application form, take part in an assessment centre exercise, and pass medical, security and reference checks. *It is important to note that each stage of the recruitment process needs to be passed for you to proceed to appointment.*

The application form

While requiring you to complete sections relating to your personal circumstances, the main focus of the application form is in relation to a series of competency based questions that are set to 'test' whether you can demonstrate the skills needed to work as a Police Community Support officer. You will be asked to provide three or four examples as evidence of these. These examples can be from a range of different sources.

It is important that you read the questions carefully so that you completely understand what is needed from you in the examples that you give and that you answer all of the questions. Take time to complete the application form and check your work fully for punctuation, grammatical and spelling errors.

The assessment centre

Within the assessment centre, which last approximately half a day, there are a series of activities and exercises that you will be required to take part in. These will include:

- Two interactive role-play exercises. These last approximately five minutes each.
- Two written exercises. These last approximately twenty minutes each.
- A structured interview. This interview is competency based and will comprise four separate questions.

If you are successful at this stage you will be required to take part in a medical and following this you would be appointed and offered a post.

Becoming a Special Constable in England and Wales

The Special Constabulary has a long and rich history within the Police, and despite many misconceptions the history of the Special Constabulary pre-dates the role of the Police Officer/Constable. The main role of a Special Constable is to add value to, and support the work of, the regular constabulary.

Reflection point

Special Constables have a specific role in the work of the Police as they are not paid and they volunteer their time to work. As a result of the powers that Special Constables have, they can be described as volunteer Police Officers. You will however be required to commit to working as a Special Constable for a minimum of four hours a week. They have the same powers as regular officers and wear the same uniforms.

What a Special Constable may be required to do (policecouldyou.co.uk)

- provide security at a range of different events;
- provide evidence in a court setting;
- enforce road safety;
- conduct foot patrols;
- tackle anti-social behaviour;
- enforce the law.

Training is ongoing and the more experience you have the more responsibility you will have.

Special Constable, 'I joined the Specials because I wanted to learn what it was like to be a Police Officer. I felt that it would help me make a decision about my future. I wasn't wrong ... it did. I would recommend anyone considering working as a Police Officer in the future to apply.'

Special Constable, 'A typical day for me as special starts at around 3pm. This means that I can go to university in the morning. After a briefing in the station with some of the regular officers I am out on patrol. Some days are quiet but others can be really hectic ... answering calls, responding to incidents, and calming down situations. It is never dull. .... Some days I could finish about 10pm or later depending upon what has happened.'

Skills and attributes required to be a Special Constable

The skills and attributes that you will be required to evidence as a Special Constable are similar to those of a regular Police Officer:

- integrity
- honesty
- ability to communicate with a wide range of people
- ability to act tactfully.

> ### Reflection point
>
> Reflect on the different activities that the Police are required to be involved in.
>
> What skills do you have that would enable you to fulfil these roles as a Special Constable?
>
> What skills will you need to develop?

The application process

The Police Service, regardless of the area that you may choose to work in, welcomes applications from a variety of different backgrounds. You must be 18 to apply and you will need to be physically fit.

As each local Police area is responsible for their own recruitment practice, the application process may vary from area to area. It is likely however that the process will be competency based and will involve a written application form, a questionnaire (competency based), an interview and an eyesight and fitness tests.

> ### Reflection point
>
> The application process to become a Special is similar in both its stages and focus to that of a regular Police Officer so you would benefit from reading that section in this chapter and revisit what you have read in the introductory chapters of this text.
>
> The College of Policing is also a useful source of information with a range of practice materials for you to have a go at.

Once appointed you would be invited to undergo a period of formal training to educate you in the work of the Police before you started your formal duty as a Special Constable.

A number of Special Constables were asked to identify what they liked about their job and what they weren't so keen on. Here are a selection of their responses.

Three things that I like about my job:

(1) A sense of paying back and helping out the local community in which I live in.

(2) The range of people who I have met, whether this be the other special constables, regular constables and staff of higher ranks, or the people who I come into contact with when on duty in the local areas.

(3) The excitement and unpredictability that every shift will entail.

Three things that I'm not quite so keen on:

(1) The sometimes unsociable hours that I work.

(2) The instant dislike from certain people when dressed in the Police uniform.

(3) The insight it gives us into how depraved and corrupt some people's lives are whom we deal with.

The structure of policing in Scotland

It is important to note here that Scotland has a separate and quite distinct legal system and structure to England and Wales and so the Justice sector is also different.

The Police Service in Scotland is part of the Justice Department and has a long and rich history. Since April 2013, however, the Police Service in Scotland became a single unified force and is known as *Police Scotland*. This change occurred as a result of the Police and Fire Reform (Scotland) Act 2012. Police Scotland is now responsible for the work of the Police across the whole of Scotland.

The work of the Police in Scotland is divided into three main areas: local policing; crime and operational support; and Commonwealth Games and major events. As a member of staff in the organisation you may be required to work in one or all of these areas.

The Police Service operationally is divided into 14 different policing areas and a commander leads all these. It is the commander's responsibility to lead the area and prioritise the policing response in accordance with local need.

The work of Police Scotland is outlined in the Annual Police Plan produced. This annual plan clearly states that its purpose is to improve the safety and wellbeing of communities in Scotland by keeping its people safe. Take time to have a look at the annual plan and familiarise yourself with the priorities and targets set. As a priority, Police Scotland operates on the principle of policing by consent.

Police staff within the 14 policing areas fulfil a variety of different roles. Vacancies for jobs are advertised via the Police Scotland website, job centres and in the local media and are usually available for a two week period.

Action point

Go onto the website and subscribe to the vacancy notification service. Full details of how to do this are given on the website.

Reflection point

The recruitment and selection processes in Scotland are aimed at identifying the 'best' people to do the job. To be eligible to apply you need to be able to meet a set of criteria. If you do not meet these criteria you will not be eligible to apply. These criteria are fully explained on the Police Scotland website. It is important that you check these criteria especially where educational qualifications are required.

Becoming a Police Officer in Scotland

Police Scotland clearly states in its literature that the role of a Police Officer requires a great deal of commitment and in reward for high standards you will be supported in the work that you do. The Police Code of Ethics provides information regarding the expectations of staff and the values that Police staff are expected to work to; these are fairness, integrity and respect.

> ## Reflection point
>
> It can be difficult to know what our value base may be, but it is very important to understand that if you don't know your values and work with something that is against what you believe this will cause you stress.
>
> Think about: what you value – why you value it . . . continue asking questions so you can understand what it is you really do value.

The role of a Police Officer in Scotland is both demanding and diverse. Police Officers work in a variety of different capacities but all work in partnership with their local communities and other parts of the Criminal Justice sector to assist in reducing crime and protecting the public. As a Police Officer a variety of different and specialist roles are available and these are all available to those who have completed their period of 'probation'.

> *Human resources*, 'Remember that you can only apply to one area at a time. Applications will not be considered if an application to another area has been made.'

As a Police Officer working in Scotland you will receive a wide range of benefits: flexible working hours, paid overtime as appropriate and around 22 days leave. The starting salary at the time of writing is around £23,493 and this salary is incremental, rising with each year of experience. Your salary will also increase to £26,223 following completion of your 2-year probationary period. Dependent upon your position you can expect your salary to increase to around £41,000 for a sergeant and £50,000 for an inspector. Within the Police there is a clearly defined promotional structure and you will be supported internally with these applications. As a Police Officer you will usually work a 40-hour week. This will be organised in different shift patterns.

Key competencies needed to become a Police Officer in Scotland

Police Scotland has clear documentation that relates to the job specification, job description and competency requirements you will need to evidence in order to be successful during the recruitment process.

- effective communication
- personal effectiveness
- teamwork
- respect for diversity
- job knowledge
- personal awareness
- problem solving
- service delivery
- leadership
- partnership working.

Action point

There are two very important skills that are essential to the Police Officer Role: effective communication and personal effectiveness. Consider how you can demonstrate your understanding of these.

Police Scotland provides full descriptors for each of the competencies stated so when considering how you could evidence the competencies refer to these.

The application process

The application process to become a Police Officer in Scotland involves the applicant meeting the requirements placed on them in a series of stages. The first stage is that of a *written application form*. This application form is aimed at ensuring that you meet the eligibility criteria and that you are able to evidence the qualities that you have which will enable you to become a Police Officer. It is important during this stage that you ensure that you provide examples from 'real situations'. These need not necessarily be linked to Police work.

If you are successful at this stage you will be invited to sit a *'standard entrance test'*. This test focuses on numeracy, literacy and information handling. Again you need to be successful at this stage to be invited to the *initial interview*. The initial interview is the point in the recruitment process where you can make a real impression.

> *P*olice Officer involved in recruitment, 'Candidates need to make sure that they know how to conduct themselves during an interview. There answers need to be structured and they need to answer the question. So many people fail at this stage because they do not answer the question.'

Following the interview you will be invited to an *Assessment Centre*. As part of this day you will take part in three separate exercises and another formal interview.

If you are successful at all stages you will be offered a position and will be fully supported through the 'probationary period' of two years.

Reflection point

Police Scotland includes in its advice and guidance section on becoming a Police Officer a range of supporting materials that can be downloaded. These materials provide the information you will need to fully familiarise yourself with the recruitment process.

Becoming a Police Leader in Scotland

There are both graduate and non-graduate entry routes to becoming a Police Leader in Scotland. These are similar to those within England and Wales, so please refer to that section of this chapter.

Becoming a Special Constable in Scotland

Reflection point

As a Special Constable in Scotland you will work alongside the regular Police in a voluntary capacity. Special Constables are described by Police Scotland as 'a positive force for change' (Police Scotland, March 2014).

Working as a Special Constable in Scotland is the same in both focus and recruitment process to that of a Special Constable in England and Wales. We refer you therefore to the relevant section earlier in the chapter.

A job specification, person specification and personal competency descriptors are available on the Police Scotland website.

There is not an equivalent role for a Police Community Support Officer in Scotland.

The structure of policing in Northern Ireland

The Police Service Northern Ireland does not at the time of writing recruit either Police Community Support Officers or Special Constables. This section of the chapter, after discussing the structure of the Police Service of Northern Ireland, will focus on the role of a Police Officer only.

Reflection point

The Police Service of Northern Ireland (PSNI) is the Police Service that governs the practice of the Police in Northern Ireland. It is important to note that this service was formed in 2001 following an Independent Commission on Policing in Northern Ireland that replaced the Royal Ulster Constabulary (RUC).

If you want to find out more look at the Police Service of Northern Ireland website.

Within Northern Ireland, at the time of writing, the Police Service is split into 10 separate departments, all with an overall responsibility for delivering the work of the Police. The *District Policing Command* is the department that deals more directly with operational work of the Police. Within this department there are eight distinct districts and these districts cover the entirety of Northern Ireland. Each of these separate districts has a Chief Superintendent and each area is led by a Chief Inspector. The Police Service of Northern Ireland states clearly that their purpose is to 'Make Northern Ireland safer for everyone through professional, progressive policing. We achieve this goal through policing with the community. This proactive, community-driven approach sees the Police and local community working together to identify and solve problems' (PSNI 2014).

In addition to the above statement The Police Service Northern Ireland (2014) also clearly outline their ambition, guiding principles and commitments.

Our ambition

To be the finest personal, professional and protective Police Service in the world

Our guiding principles

To be personal, impartial and accountable Police Officers and staff
To make a difference
To be responsible and flexible
To have appropriately targeted resources
To challenge the status quo
To provide value for money
To work in partnership with other agencies and sectors

Action point

How would these principles apply to the work that you would do as a Police Officer?

Our commitments

To design and implement clear policing commitments
To put communities and victims first
To serve every individual regardless of – religion, politics, cultural
    identity, age, gender or sexual orientation.

*The Police Ombudsman for Northern Ireland and The
Northern Ireland Policing Board oversee the work of the
Northern Ireland Police.*

The Police Service Northern Ireland, at the time of writing,
employs around 7,000 full time Police Officers and around 2,500
support staff. There are a variety of roles available within the
Police and there is a stated commitment to employing civilians.
The recruitment process for all employees is set around assessing
skills and experience and as such is competency based (PSNI
2014).

Action point

Employment within the sector is advertised in a variety of
places but full information can be obtained on the Grafton
Recruitments website. Access the website and look at the
information available.

Action point

When you are considering your career choices into the Police
Service you would benefit from completing some voluntary
work experience in the Criminal Justice sector; although not
essential it is desirable and would place you at an advantage
when identifying and demonstrating skills and competencies.

Becoming a Police Officer in Northern Ireland

The role of a Police Officer in Northern Ireland is both demanding and diverse. Police Officers work in a variety of different

capacities but all work in partnership with their local communities and other parts of the Criminal Justice sector to assist in reducing crime and protecting the public. As a Police Officer, a variety of different and specialist roles are available and these are all available to those who have completed their period of 'probation'.

As a Police Officer working in Northern Ireland you will receive a wide range of benefits, flexible working hours, paid overtime as appropriate and around 22 days leave. The starting salary at the time of writing is around £23,259 and this salary is incremental, rising with each year of experience. Within the Police there is a clearly defined promotional structure and you will be supported internally with these applications. As a Police Officer you will usually work a 40-hour week. This will be organised in different shift patterns.

In return for this the Police Service in Northern Ireland are clear about the expectations that they have of the applicants and their staff.

You will be required to:

- work unsociable hours;
- wear a uniform at all times;
- undertake a 22 week training programme;
- demonstrate a commitment to continual professional development;
- work anywhere in Northern Ireland;
- pass a physical fitness test.

Reflection point

You need to be able to demonstrate your physical fitness. The Police Service Northern Ireland requires you to be able to run, crawl, lift, carry and cycle. There is a clear training programme, which they recommend that you follow before you apply to ensure that you are physically fit. Check on the Police Service Northern Ireland for full details.

> *P*olice Officer, 'Flexibility is important. If you want a 9–5 job then don't apply.'

The application process

At the time of writing there are no active recruitment campaigns. The process described below is therefore only to act as a guide as this may change in future campaigns.

Reflection point

The application process to become a Police Officer in Northern Ireland is similar both in the various stages and also in relation to what needs to be evidenced to those of a Police Officer in England and Wales and in Scotland; please refer to the earlier sections on Policing in England and Wales and Scotland for information regarding the various stages and exercises that relate to the process and for further things to consider. It is also important that you refer to the earlier chapters in this text, especially Chapter 4.

Becoming a Police Leader in Northern Ireland

There are both graduate and non-graduate entry routes to becoming a Police Leader in Northern Ireland. These are similar to those within England and Wales and Scotland so please refer to that section of this chapter. The Police Service Northern Ireland does however have a *High Potential Development Scheme* that operates as a structured career development framework. This scheme is available to all Police Officers who demonstrate drive and determination. The scheme is based on competencies and linked to academic learning. This learning is related to leadership and management skills. The literature regarding the programme states clearly that the skills needing to be evidence in a rigorous and demanding process are:

- leadership skills
- decision-making skills
- management skills
- adaptability
- resilience
- ability to deliver results despite the challenge.

Action point

Look at the skills listed above. It is important that you think about these and most importantly how you will evidence them.

There are different stages to the recruitment process and these include the completion of an application form, a written test and an assessment centre process that incorporates an interview.

Action point

To assist you in preparing for this recruitment process there are a number of different resources available online and we would suggest that you take time to have a look at these and practise them. Do not worry too much if the tests are not in a related field to the Police Service, it's the practice that is important and remember that the tests are not designed to have a correct answer but require you to evaluate the most appropriate response from those presented. Knowing your agency and organisation is important.

working in the police   157

Chapter summary

This chapter has considered the different roles that are available within the Police Services in the UK. Within the chapter the authors have focussed on the roles and the recruitment and selection processes relating to the role of a Police Officer, a Police Community Support Officer, A Special Constable and that of a Police Leader. Included throughout the chapters are action and reflection tasks that you will have thought about and completed. Finally some top tips from the chapter have been included. We hope that you have enjoyed reading the chapter and that you are more informed about what you will need to do to secure a job within this part of the sector should you choose to apply.

Top tips

- Think of your contribution to a team.
- How do you know you have communicated effectively?
- How do you make your degree relevant?
- What is the core focus of your dissertation/work-based learning project?
- How can you evidence your skills?
- Understand the organisation.
- Take time to read and familiarise yourself with the recruitment process.
- Give yourself time to complete the application form correctly.
- Practise your communication skills.
- Understand the assessment criteria.
- Know the difference between essential and desirable selection criteria.
- Practise your presentation skills; including your non-verbal communication.

- Be aware of your values and motivations.
- Think about why you want the job that you have applied for.

Some useful websites

- www.justice.gov.uk (The website of the Ministry of Justice)
- www.policecouldyou.co.uk (The website covering all aspects of Police recruitment)
- www.police.uk (Police information)
- www.college.police.uk (The website of the College of Policing)
- www.gov.uk (The website covering government services in England and Wales)
- www.prospects.ac.uk (The official graduate careers website)
- www.sfjuk.com (The website of the sector skills council Skills for Justice)
- www.policespecials.com (The website for information regarding the role of a Special and the recruitment process)
- www.merseyside.police.uk (The website of Merseyside Police)
- www.psni.police.uk (The website of the Police Service of Northern Ireland)
- www.scotland.police.uk (The website of Police Scotland)

Recommended reading

There are a wide range of readings that you could refer to but the recommendations below provide a broad overview.

Cox, P. (2007) *Passing the Recruit Assessment Process*. Exeter: Learning Matters

Joyce, P. (2010) *Policing: Development and contemporary practice*. London: Sage

Malthouse, R., Kennard, P. and Roffey-Barentsen, J. (2009) *Interactive Exercises for the Police Recruit Assessment Process: Succeeding at role plays*. Exeter: Learning Matters

Newburn, T. (Ed.)(2004) *Policing: Key readings*. Cullompton: Willan Publishing

Pepper, I. (2011) *Working in Policing*. Exeter: Learning Matters

Policing Matters Series, published by www.learningmatters.co.uk – a series of books concerning policing issues.

Rogers, C., Lewis, R., John, T. and Read, T. (2011) *Police Work: Principles and practice*. London: Routledge

Williams, P., Blake, C. and Sheldon, B. (2010) *Policing and Criminal Justice*. London: Sage

References

Police Act (1996) Schedule 4. Retrieved from www.legislation.gov.uk/ukpa/1996/16/schedule/4 (accessed 27 May 2014)

Prospects (2014, January) Police officer: job description. Retrieved from www.prospects.ac.uk/police_officer_job_description.htm (accessed 7 August 2014)

Skills for Justice (2009) *Skills for Justice Labour Market Information Report for Adult Advancement Career Service*. Retrieved from www.sfjuk.com (accessed 7 August 2014)

Wright, A. (2002) *Policing: An introduction to concepts and practice*. Devon: Willan

chapter 7

Working in prisons

Chapter objectives

By the end of this chapter you should be able to:

■ understand the key issues/drivers within the Prison System;

■ understand the way that the Prison Service operates in England and Wales, Scotland and Northern Ireland;

■ identify the range of roles available within the Prison Service;

■ identify the different stages of the recruitment process for the following roles: a Prison Officer and a Prison Manager in England and Wales, Scotland and Northern Ireland.

Introduction to the Prison Service

The Prison Service is the part of the Criminal Justice System that works to keep those individuals sent by the courts in custody, as a convicted or remanded prisoner. Prisons are an integral part of society and something that most of us take for granted. The Prison Service, either public or private within the UK, is clear in all of its documentation that its duty is to keep those in custody and to do this with humanity, and to work towards those incarcerated leading law-abiding lives both while serving their sentence and upon their release back into the community. As with many other sectors in the Criminal Justice System the Prison Service has a commitment to working in a multi-disciplinary way, both within the prison and with its stakeholders in the community.

It is important when considering a career in the Prison Service that you also consider the factors, changes and influences that the Prison Service has been subject to in recent years and how this may impact on the role you will have. You would benefit from reading more in depth texts recommended at the end of the chapter, and in referring back to Chapter 2 of this text for more in depth knowledge.

Action point

Review what you have read about the Prison Service in Chapter 2 of this text. Note down some of the key points raised from the chapter and think about their implications for you working in the Prison Service.

In introducing the reader to the institution of the prison, this chapter will begin by providing a *brief overview* of the Prison Service and its current position in the Criminal Justice System. This is important because, for most of us, the prison is an invisible world, upon which we base our attitudes and opinions on the images created in the media or discussed by politicians. Importantly here the *vision*, *objectives* and *principles* of the Prison Service will be highlighted. *Key figures* will also be provided in relation to the number of prison establishments, the numbers of people incarcerated and the numbers of people working within the prison estate. The chapter will then move on to consider the range of roles and careers available within the Prison Service and in doing so the competencies, skills and values required working within this sector. Within this chapter the careers discussed will be those of a *Prison Officer*, a *Prison*

Manager and the *graduate managerial* schemes that lead to accelerated promotions and prison management. These careers have been chosen because they provide insight into the natural career progression through the service and also because of the feedback received from students currently studying on related degree programmes. The *entry requirements* and *application process* will be considered for each role before moving through to a more general analysis of the *skills* needed to be successful in securing employment within the Prison System.

Action point

When you are considering your career choices into the Prison Service you would benefit from completing some voluntary work experience in the Criminal Justice sector, although not essential it is desirable and would place you at an advantage when identifying and demonstrating skills and competencies.

Throughout the chapter there will be a focus on providing *practical advice* and *guidance* to assist you in beginning to develop an awareness of what working within a prison environment is like, what career opportunities are available, what skills and knowledge you will need to work in the environment and to hopefully dispel any myths that you may have.

Reflection point

We need to acknowledge that the term 'prisoner' is used throughout this chapter. The courts use it because it is a label that has been ascribed to an individual who has been deprived of their liberty because of a decision made.

Think about how you feel about the label 'prisoner'. Do you agree with it or not? Are there other terms that could be better suited to describe someone detained within a prison environment?

Within the chapter, a distinction will be made between the systems, recruitment processes and practice in England and Wales, Scotland and Northern Ireland. Again it is important that you consider these differences and the implications of them for the area and role that you wish to work in. You may, as a result of increasing your knowledge about the different areas, also broaden your horizons about where you could work in the future.

Throughout the chapter you will recognise similarities between the practice and processes of recruitment in England and Wales, Scotland and Northern Ireland. The linked action, reflection points and comments from those working in the sector are therefore important for you to consider in their entirety.

Action point

Have a look at the different Prison Service websites for England and Wales, Scotland and Northern Ireland and write down the different roles that are available. What are the differences between the areas?

Brief general overview of the Prison Service

The Prison Service, as with many other parts of the Criminal Justice System, is constantly evolving and developing not only in relation to its structure and organisation but also in relation to the focus of the work that it does. In gaining an understanding of the Prison Service as it is today, and what it may be like to work within it, it is important to first look at its history and development. It is important to note at the start of this section that rates of imprisonment in the United Kingdom and within England and Wales specifically are one of the highest in Western Europe (Ministry of Justice, January 2014) and that this shows no sign of changing.

The Prison Service, as we know it today, has evolved over a period of 300 years and since its imposition has progressed through many changes and developments. Traditionally prisons were used as a place to 'hold' people awaiting punishment or trial. They were rarely used as a place of punishment. Throughout the eighteenth and nineteenth century many changes occurred within the Prison System and new ideas related to reform and rehabilitation began to emerge. In relation to these changes there have been a number of key individuals, such as John Howard, Elizabeth Fry and William Brebner who campaigned for the conditions in the Prison System to be addressed. It is interesting to note here that these changes influenced the status that was given to those who worked within the Prison System and the emergence of the prison governor led to the gradual imposition of improved working conditions, training and holiday entitlements for those who worked in the system. These ideas have continued into the twentieth and twenty-first century with a renewed focus on resettlement and desistance.

The *three main legal uses* of the Prison System have in one form or another been custodial, punishment and coercion. It is important to consider these when looking at the way in which the Prison System has developed.

Custodial: People are kept in prison while they are waiting their sentence/punishment or their trial.

Punishment: People are kept in prison because they have been given a sentence for an offence that has been committed.

Coercion: People are kept in prison because they have failed to complete/comply with an order or punishment of the court.

It is important when you are considering a career in this sector that you give some time and thought to who the 'prisoners' are and do not see them as a single homogenous group. The Prison Reform Trust is a useful source of statistical information relating to the social and economic groupings within the Prison System. The statistics that you will come across paint quite a worrying picture about those that are imprisoned. It is also important that you consider the Criminal Justice makeup of prisoners, i.e. those on remand or those sentenced, as this is also varied.

An important development within this sector has been the introduction of private prisons. The introduction of private prisons began in 1992 when a number of prisons began to be built publically but then run privately. All private prisons are subject to a system of control that links them to the National Offender Management Service and the HM Chief Inspectorate of Prisons inspects the private institutions in the same way that it would public prisons. The organisations involved in the contractual management of the private vary according to where they are in the UK but some examples of those organisations are Serco and G4S Justice Services.

A range of different pieces of legislation governs the Prison Service. Again it is important for you to consider the relevant legislation, as they will impact on the role that you have and on the delivery of services within the prison estate.

The Prison Service in England and Wales

The structure of the Prison Service in England and Wales

The Ministry of Justice website clearly lays out the vision, objectives and principles of the Prison Service and it is important when looking for a career within this sector that you are aware of these. The National Archives of HM Prison Service also has links to other areas that relate to its corporate structure such as security, decency, and equality and diversity.

Our vision:

- to provide the very best Prison Service so that we are the provider of choice;
- to work towards this vision by securing the following key objectives.

Our objectives:

To protect the public and provide what commissioners want to purchase by:

- holding prisoners securely;
- reducing the risk of prisoners re-offending;
- providing safe and well-ordered establishments in which we treat prisoners humanely, decently and lawfully.

In securing these objectives we adhere to the following principles:

Our principles:

In carrying out work we:

- work in close partnership with our commissioners and others in the Criminal Justice System to achieve common objectives;
- obtain best value from the resources available using research to ensure effective correctional practice;
- promote diversity, equality of opportunity and combat unlawful discrimination;
- ensure our staff have the right leadership, organisation, support and preparation to carry out their work effectively.

It is important when looking at the Prison System in England and Wales that you are aware of some key facts and figures.

Key Facts (Bromley Briefings 2013)

- 142 prisons in the UK
- 139 prisons in England and Wales
- 14 private prisons

- 19 new prisons built since 1995 in England and Wales
- 7 of these are run privately in England and Wales
- current male prison population is 80,741
- current female prison population is 3,892
- 58 children in custody aged 10–14
- 77,595 people working in custodial care
- approx. 85 per cent workforce in England and Wales
- public sector employs around 85 per cent of the workforce.

Becoming a Prison Officer in England and Wales

Prison Officers within England and Wales work in a variety of different capacities and institutions, however all Prison Officers work directly with prisoners in prisons, remand centres or young offender institutions. The work of a Prison Officer will vary depending upon where they work, the type of prison and the category of the prison, but their work will always involve more than just ensuring that prisoners obey the rules of the prison/establishment (these rules vary from prison to prison).

*P*rison Officer, 'Candidates need to be aware of how diverse the job can be. No two days are the same.'

As a Prison Officer a variety of different roles are available and you could be involved in the education and training of prisoners, their health and welfare, preparing prisoners for their release, resettlement, and their offending behaviour. It is important when looking at the role in greater detail that you link the vision, objectives and principles with your own.

Reflection point

Do you feel that you would be suited to some of these roles better than others? Why?

In addition to these duties an essential skill for a Prison Officer is their ability to think on their feet and make quick decisions. In addition *six key behavioural skills* are identified for being successful as a Prison Officer and these are:

Non-verbal communication

This skill includes the appropriate use of body language such as maintaining eye contact, using gestures and effectively listening and engaging.

Showing understanding

This skill relates to you demonstrating that you understand and can differentiate between different situations. Your ability to listen effectively is important here.

Suspending judgement

This skill relates to the decisions and the judgements that you make and importantly in this your ability to time these decisions appropriately.

Being assertive

This skill relates to you being able to demonstrate the 'correct' behaviour in a given situation. It requires you to demonstrate that you can maintain balance and be able to argue a point without becoming aggressive. Staying calm is crucial here.

Respect for diversity

This skill requires you to be able to show your respect for the differences between people and to be able to challenge any comments or stereotypes. This requires you to be able to address issues concerning race, gender, age, sexuality, religion, class, ability/disability, language etc.

Exploring and clarifying

This skill means that you can ask appropriate questions for the task and to understand the issues involved.

Some typical work activities may include: performing security checks, supervising prisoners, carrying out personal officer duties, escorting prisoners, advising prisoners, and liaising with other staff and organisations both within the prison and the community.

The role is therefore varied, demanding and dynamic and while offering many challenges also brings with it a lot of rewards and further career opportunities. By taking time to read this chapter and researching the role further you will greatly increase your chances of becoming a Prison Officer.

*P*rison Manager, 'It is important that you enjoy working with people, enjoy variety and that you are adaptable.'

Entry requirements

In England and Wales, individual institutions carry out their own recruitment. Vacancies are advertised locally in Jobcentres, the local press and through the Prison Service website (see 'Some useful websites' for details). In Scotland, recruitment is carried out centrally at the Prison Service headquarters.

It is also important to look at whether the prison you are applying to is publically or privately run. Within this section the more general entry requirements are outlined. Where differences apply to the recruitment process these will be highlighted.

To be considered for a Prison Officer role you will need:

* to be between 18–62;
* to be a UK or Commonwealth citizen, a EU national, a foreign national with granted stay permissions or have been resident in the UK for three years;
* to declare any criminal convictions;
* to be able to pass a medical, eyesight and a fitness test.

Reflection point

Think about these criteria and whether you are able to meet them. As part of this reflection point look at the criteria set specifically for the medical, eyesight and fitness test on the Prison Service website.

The Prison Service values applications from a range of people and the experience that you may previously have had such as in the armed forces or a related profession such as the Police will be useful during the application stage. Practical skills such as building, joinery and engineering are also useful. In addition to the above criteria you must also be able to pass an entrance test known as the Prison Officer Selection Test (POST). Information regarding this test will be discussed later in the chapter. A degree is only essential if you are considering applying for the National Offender Management Service (NOMS) Graduate Programme. This programme will be discussed later in this chapter.

As a Prison Officer you will usually work a 39-hour week. This will be organised in different shift patterns, dependent upon the needs of the institution you work in. You should be prepared to work nights, weekends and days. Some prisons operate a self-roistering shift pattern so that there is some flexibility for staff. The starting salary at the time of writing is approx. £18,000, although this can vary according to the institution you are working in.

Reflection point

Consider the implications this may have on your lifestyle. Would this suit you?

The application process

Prison Officer jobs are advertised in a variety of places, including the local media and online. The Ministry of Justice website has good links to available vacancies via its vacancy search tool. The G4S website also has vacancies listed. If there are no current vacancies listed, it is advisable to register your interest for any future opportunities that may arise.

> *riminal Justice student*, 'Registering with the site gave me a 'heads up' on the jobs when they became available. Do this sooner rather than later.'

There are various stages to the application process and these will now be discussed.

Eligibility questions

If you meet the minimum eligibility criteria as outlined earlier in this chapter your application will be formally acknowledged. Following this you will be invited to sit a *Prison Officer Selection Test*.

Prison Officer Selection Test (POST)

This test is an online test that tests the applicant's literacy, numeracy and reasoning skills. No prior knowledge of the work of a Prison Officer is required at this stage as this test is more focussed on your common sense when answering questions. As part of this test there are around 50–60 questions and you have an hour to complete the questions once you have started. Success at this stage determines whether your application proceeds further. Those that are successful are invited to take part in a Recruitment Assessment Day or, if for a private sector organisation such as G4S, a formal and structured interview.

This test will require you to demonstrate your *listening skills, writing skills, reading skills, recalling information skills* and *reading comprehension skills*.

Action point

Take time to have a look at the information available online regarding the content of these tests and practise, practise, practise.

Recruitment Assessment Day (RAD)

This part of the application process is concerned with assessing the candidate's aptitude for the role as a Prison Officer and, in a variety of role-plays and tests, the skills required will also be addressed. During the day you will be required to take part in a numeracy test, a language test, a fitness test and finally a medical test. These tests are all part of the assessment of your suitability as a Prison Officer. You will be required to evidence a range of skills, as the purpose of all the activities is to determine how you would respond to situations that you might have to face in practice.

It is important here that you take time to consider the behavioural skills as discussed earlier in this chapter and relate these to the following:

- your potential for leadership
- your ability to act professionally
- your ability to learn from others
- your ability to be a team player
- your communication skills
- your people skills
- your awareness of the role of prisons in the broader Criminal Justice System
- your ability to act responsibly
- your awareness of broader societal issues
- your ability to be adaptable.

Prison Manager, 'Candidates don't always realise that they have to evidence these skills. Evidence is more than just saying what you did. This is one of the main reasons that candidates are not successful.'

As part of the Recruitment Assessment Day you will be required to take part in a structured interview. The questions will be focussed around the skills and values needed to be an effective Prison Officer. One of the managers we spoke to while preparing this chapter stated that the interview would likely include a question on team working, dealing with challenging behaviours, diversity and an industry related question.

It is important to note here that for Prison Officer posts within the private sector the Recruitment Assessment Day may not apply and the focus will be mainly on the formal interview process.

If you are successful in *all* elements of the recruitment process you will be formally appointed. If a vacancy is immediately available then you will be allocated the vacancy otherwise you should expect to be placed on a reserve/waiting list. You will remain eligible for a vacancy for a period of up to 18 months after which time you would need to apply again.

What happens once I am appointed?

Before you commence your career as a Prison Officer you will be required to embark on a training programme. The length of this training programme will differ depending upon whether you are employed by the public or private sector. However the content of the training is similar and with that in mind the next section of this chapter highlights the more general areas that will be covered in the training. The training programme can, as already stated, vary in length and this can be anywhere from one week to eight weeks. The focus of the training is to provide you with the skills, knowledge and values you will need to develop to become both competent and confident in your role. You will already have demonstrated these skills at some level through the recruitment process, so the training will be focussed on the development of these. Initially your training will start with an induction programme, which may be at the institution you have been allocated to. The focus of this part of the training is familiarisation with the prison, prisoners, colleagues and management structure.

*P*rison Officer, 'I was surprised by how much writing was involved in the job. Everything you do needs to be recorded.'

The training then develops into focussing on specific areas that are more skill based. This part of the training takes place away from the institution. You will be required to engage in

working in prisons

competency-based role-plays, class-based learning, team-building exercises, and control and restraint. Within the training programme assessments are incorporated including written based assessments. The final part of the training will be back at the institution and is focussed on you contextualising what you have learnt before you fully go into 'operational life' as a Prison Officer.

Action point

Have a look at the CCNVQ in custodial care. What does the course entail? What would you be required to study?

Becoming a Prison Service Manager in England and Wales

Within the Prison Service there are many opportunities for career progression both in the variety of roles available but also in relation to promotion to management level grades. While many managers reach the positions internally you can always apply directly for management positions without having been a Prison Officer.

You can become a Prison Service Manager as a non-graduate. There are different career routes within the public and private sector prisons but both involve different levels of management, with different levels of responsibility that lead eventually to director grades. It is important to look at these promotion routes and the roles and responsibilities that apply to them.

Skills required for promotion to management levels:

- staff management skills
- observational skills
- decision-making skills
- common sense skills
- interpersonal skills
- innovative thinking skills.

*P*rison Manager, 'My job as a prison leader/manager requires me to be versatile and adaptable. I need to be able to diffuse situations when they arise and be able to stay calm and controlled.'

Both the public sector and the private sector offer graduate level managerial schemes and again it is important that you look at the details of the programmes available. Within this chapter the authors have chosen to focus on the National Offender Management Service graduate programme as an example of the schemes.

National Offender Management Service graduate programme

The National Offender Management Service graduate programme is aimed specifically at those graduates who want to become *prison leaders*. The programme will see you develop from your first role as a Prison Officer, through to a Supervisor Officer level, a Custodial Manager and finally an Operational Manager, where you will be required to manage a particular area of a prison. At each stage of this process you will be supported and mentored.

Reflection point

A prison leader is a term used by the Prison Service. Prison leaders are seen as role models to their colleagues, prisoners in their care and the community. What is the importance of this for the work you would do in this capacity?

It is crucial at this stage that you consider the qualities that National Offender Management Service states that Prison

Managers should have. These are broken down into two distinct categories. First the *type of person* you are and second *the skills* you will need to evidence.

Reflection point

Type of person

- adaptable
- resilient
- decisive
- calm
- focussed
- rational
- logical
- enjoy variety
- principled
- adaptable.

Skills needed

- ability to work professionally
- ability to work with others
- ability to achieve results
- ability to problem solve
- ability to act with integrity
- ability to persuade and influence
- ability to communicate effectively
- ability to embrace change
- ability to develop self and others
- ability to work in a team
- ability to show respect for others.

The recruitment process

The recruitment and selection of individuals for the *prison leaders programme* is a demanding one and requires you to be able to evidence *your skills*, *abilities*, *values* and *aptitudes* in a variety of different contexts. To be eligible to apply you must be a graduate with a 2.1 or above or be in your final year with an expectation of achieving that grade. The starting salary is in the region of £26,000 and each year there are about 10–15 opportunities available.

There are different stages to the recruitment process and these include a short application form, an online situational judgement test, an online numerical reasoning test, a job simulation day, a written assessment and interview, and finally a medical and fitness examination. You will also be required to pass a security clearance.

It is important to note that you need to be *successful at each stage* of the recruitment process to be appointed. This chapter will now consider some of the key points from each of these stages.

Application form

When completing the application form you *must* ensure that you fill in all of the sections that are required and you do this as comprehensively as asked. Take time to complete the application form and check your work fully for punctuation, grammatical and spelling errors.

Reflection point

Do I need to improve on my spelling, punctuation and grammar?

Online tests

The online tests that are set are used to establish your suitability for the job based on the skills and competencies required. You should link these to the exercise above.

In the *Situational Judgement Test* you will be presented with a variety of work situations that you may encounter if you were appointed. In each of these situations you will be required to choose or rate the different options presented for each situation in relation to how effective they would be to deal with the situation(s) presented. Confidence and the ability to address situations from a variety of different perspectives are crucial success factors. In relation to this test and the scenarios set no previous prison experience is required, however we would argue that gaining some experience either in a voluntary or paid capacity would be beneficial.

Action point

To assist you in preparing for this test there are a number of different resources available online and we would suggest that you take time to have a look at these and practise them. Do not worry too much if the tests are not in a related field to the Prison Service, it's the practice that is important and remember that the tests are not designed to have a correct answer but require you to evaluate the most appropriate response from those presented. Knowing your agency and organisation is important.

The *Numerical Reasoning Test* is designed to test your understanding of different types of numerical data, statistics and your ability to make logical decisions. The numerical reasoning test is at present co-ordinated by an organisation called SHL.

Action point

Take time to have a look at the SHL website and familiarise yourself with the types of questions that are asked. Again practice is the key. If maths is not your strong point take a look at the GCSE BiteSize Maths website.

> '*R*emember you may be tested again at the end of the recruitment process so cheating is not recommended.'

Job Simulation Assessment Centre (JSAC)

This part of the recruitment process is designed to test the applicant's aptitude for a future prison leader. Within the JASC you will be presented with four role-play exercises. Each of these exercises is designed with the core identified prison leader behaviours in mind. These include: *non-verbal listening skills, demonstrating understanding, assertiveness, ability to explore and clarify, ability to suspend judgement* and *your respect for diversity*.

Action point

Look at the skills listed above. It is important that you think about these and importantly how you will evidence them.

Each of the scenarios you take part in will be filmed and will be watched as it takes place. The recording of the scenarios acts as a measure of quality control and ensures that all candidates in the process are treated consistently.

Written paper and interview

The written paper and the interview are the final stages in the process of recruitment. Each year about 50 applicants reach this stage of the process. Both of these tests are competency based. The *written paper* focusses on problem solving, decision-making and communication skills. This test can be completed either electronically or in a hand written form. The *interview* is the final stage of the process and is your final opportunity to impress the prospective employers. The aim of the interview is to enable the employers to see how you have or would respond to situations that link to the competencies of the role.

Action point

Review the STAR method discussed in Chapter 4. Prepare answers to evidence the above skills and write these down.
Think about what the purpose of the written paper is.
Remember the importance of getting your grammar, spelling and punctuation correct.

You must pass each stage of the process to be able to progress to the next. If you are successful in *all* elements of the recruitment process you will be formally appointed.

The Prison Service in Scotland

The structure of the Prison Service in Scotland

It is important to note here that Scotland has a separate and quite distinct legal system and structure to England and Wales and so the justice sector is also different.

Action point

Review what you have read in Chapter 2 of this text as a reminder of the difference in the Scottish Legal System.

The Prison Service within Scotland is part of the Justice Department and was set up in 1993. It is an executive agency of the Scottish Government. The Cabinet Secretary for Justice governs the Prison Service within Scotland and as part of this there are five separate directorates. Information regarding these directorates can be found on the Scottish Prison Service website. The Scottish Prison Service is a public led agency and as such works to contribute towards a safer Scotland. Within its documentation the Scottish Prison Service clearly states the vision, mission, purpose, aims and values of the work that it does and it is crucial that when looking towards a career in this service that you are fully aware of these and how they will be linked to the recruitment and selection process.

Our vision

To make Scotland safer by protecting the public and reducing offending.

Our mission

- to keep in custody those committed by the courts;
- to maintain good order in each prison;
- to care for prisoners with humanity;
- to encourage prisoners to take opportunities which will reduce the likelihood they re-offend and help reintegrate them back into their community;
- to protect the public.

Our values

- respect
- integrity
- teamwork
- equality.

Our aims

- to reduce re-offending;
- to protect the public;
- to provide a service that is 'fit for purpose';

- to offer value for money;
- to work in partnership with other organisations;
- to invest in staff development so that its staff work with professionalism and skill.

> **Action point**
>
> Look at the Scottish Prison Service Corporate Plan 2012–2015 and organisational review, *Transforming Lives and Unlocking Potential*. This can be found on their website.

It is important when looking at the system in Scotland that you are aware of some key facts and figures.

Key Facts: (Scottish Prison Service, February 2014)

- 8,113 people in custodial care (expected rise to 9,500 by 2020/21)
- 16 prison establishments
- 13 public prisons
- 2 private prisons
- 1 prison only for women
- 1,086 untried adult men on remand
- 91 untried adult women on remand
- 137 young men on remand
- 3 young women on remand
- 5,491 adult sentenced men
- 285 adult sentenced women
- 344 sentenced young men
- 11 sentenced young women
- 251 convicted prisoners awaiting sentence
- 80 recalled life prisoners
- 324 prisoners on a Home Detention Curfew
- 4,514 people working in custodial care.

Working in the Scottish Prison Service

The Scottish Prison Service, in line with its mission statement, values a diverse staff group and as such encourages applications from people from all sectors of life, backgrounds and with a range of experiences. Applications are welcomed both from *graduates* and *non-graduates* alike and within this section of the chapter these will be highlighted where appropriate.

Vacancies within Scotland are advertised in a variety of places. It is important that you check the Scottish Prison Service website regularly for updates.

Differently from England and Wales, recruitment is carried out centrally at the Prison Service headquarters in Edinburgh. The Scottish Prison Service as an organisation clearly set out the eligibility and suitability requirements needed in order to work for them. It is important that you check these eligibility and suitability requirements prior to your application.

All of the Scottish Prison Service recruitment and selection practice is based on a competency framework. The competencies identified are all linked to the vision, mission and values as identified earlier.

Action point

Look at the website and the competencies framework. Write down what the competencies mean in practice and think about how you would evidence these in the recruitment process.

Following the set application process, post application checks are also carried out that focus on references, disclosure information, occupational health checks and drug testing.

If you were to be successful in gaining employment within the Scottish Prison Service you would be a Civil Servant. Within this structure there is a clearly defined pay and benefits package, which varies according to the role that you will have. Full details can be found on Scottish Prison Service website.

Action point

As an employee of the Scottish Prison Service you will be accountable to the Civil Service Code. Take time to look at this code and think about what it may mean for you in practice.

Eligibility, pay and benefits

In order to apply for a post within the Scottish Prison Service you will be required to complete the stated nationality requirements and as part of the requirements of the Rehabilitation of Offenders Act 1974 (exclusions and exceptions), (Scotland) Order 2003 (as amended) declare your criminal convictions (Scottish Prison Service, January 2014).

As an employer, the Scottish Prison Service prides itself on offering a fully inclusive and comprehensive package of benefits that includes financial reward, professional recognition, health concerns and flexible working patterns. Details regarding the particular pay and benefits for the role that you are applying for can be found on the Scottish Prison Service website.

Becoming a Prison Officer in Scotland

The Scottish Prison Service clearly states in its literature that the role of a Prison Officer requires the individual to be professional, responsible, confident and compassionate. Prison Officers within Scotland work in a variety of different capacities and institutions; however all Prison Officers work in one of two distinct roles. Main Prison Officer roles:

- operations and residential
- regimes.

Reflection point

All newly appointed Prison Officers start within the operational and residential role. As part of this role you would be required to be involved in a range of different activities that would include: gate duties, the reception of prisoners and visitors, the supervision and management of prisoners, monitoring security, dealing with requests from the public and community, and patrol duties.

Reflect on what this will mean for you in practice.

Essential skills

- communication skills
- teamwork skills
- patience and consideration skills
- resilience
- enthusiasm.

Reflection point

Review what you read in Chapter 4 of this book. Pay particular attention to the skills described, particularly resilience.

Application process

The application process has four key stages. These stages will now be discussed.

Stage 1

At this stage you will be required to complete an application form and in doing this provide evidence that relates to educational ability, skills, age, compliance with the civil service guidelines and compliance with the criminal convictions policy. At this stage of the process all of the questions asked are to be fully completed. It is important that you pay attention throughout to the competency framework identified earlier. If you meet all the requirements at this stage you will progress to Stage 2.

Stage 2

The second stage of the application process focuses on a range of different exercises as part of an Assessment Centre exercise. The Assessment Centre is not necessarily a place but a process that you will be involved in. The Assessment Centre is divided into two separate parts and is concerned with assessing your aptitude for the role as a Prison Officer, and in a variety of role-plays, tests and formal interviews the skills and competencies required will also be addressed. *You will need to pass Part 1 in order to progress.* Part 1 involves you taking part in a psycho-metric test, which includes a numerical and verbal reasoning test.

Action point

To assist you in preparing for this test there are a number of different resources available online and we would suggest that you take time to have a look at these and practise them. Do not worry too much if the tests are not in a related field to the Prison Service, it's the practice that is important and remember that the tests are not designed to have a correct answer but require you to evaluate the most appropriate response from those presented. Knowing your agency and organisation is important.

Take time to have a look at the SHL website and familiarise yourself with the types of questions that are asked in an assessment centre process. Again practice is the key. If maths is not your strong point take a look at the GCSE Bitesize Maths website.

Part 2 involves a formal interview and a fitness test. The questions in the formal interview will be competency based and will be focussed around the skills and values needed to be an effective Prison Officer.

Action point

Earlier in this chapter we focussed on things to consider when preparing for a competency based interview. Read this section and complete the linked exercise.

Stage 3

This part of the recruitment process involves the pre-employment checks being made. These are as stated earlier in the general section. If you are successful at all of the above stages you will formally appointed.

Stage 4

This final stage means that you will be eligible for a post once one is available. The availability of the posts depends upon the operational needs and requirements of the service.

> **H**uman resources, 'Keep checking the website for details of vacancies.'

Becoming a Prison Service Manager in Scotland

Within the Scottish Prison Service there are many opportunities for career progression both in the variety of roles available but also in relation to promotion to management level grades. While many managers reach the positions internally you can always apply directly for management positions without having been a Prison Officer.

Routes to becoming a Prison Service Manager can be either non-gradate or graduate.

There are different career routes within the public and private sector prisons but both involve different levels of management, with different levels of responsibility that lead eventually to director grades. It is important to look at these promotion routes and the roles and responsibilities that apply to them.

Skills required for promotion to management levels (Scottish prison Service Website, December 2013):

- staff management skills
- observational skills

- decision-making skills
- common sense skills
- interpersonal skills
- innovative thinking skills
- leadership skills
- physical fitness
- motivational skills
- listening skills.

*P*rison Manager, 'My job as a prison leader/manager requires me to be versatile and adaptable. I need to be able to diffuse situations when they arise and be able to stay calm and controlled.'

Prison Governors, or Operational Managers as they may be called, are responsible for the overall management and security of the prison in which they work.

Reflection point

Think about this level of responsibility and what it may mean in practice. How would you feel being responsible for the safety of a large number of people?

The hours of work can be long and will without doubt include evenings and weekends. It is important to note that you may be required to travel as part of this role and you may be located within a prison not in the locality where you live. The salary of a prison manager can vary so it is important that you look at where you will be appointed. The broad salary scale however is in the region of £30,000–80,000 a year. You may also be required to move for a particular job or for a promotion.

Upon appointment your initial training as a Prison Service Manager will take place at an operational place. You will usually be placed on a unit or operational wing.

As part of the route to becoming a Prison Service Manager the Scottish Prison Service offers a *Trainee Manager Programme*. This programme is aimed at *graduate level* entry and you will need to have a 2:1 Honours Degree or above be able to evidence a minimum of 12 months' related work experience and be able to demonstrate and evidence the following skills: ability to build positive working relationships, to be able to work effectively with others, to be a capable leader and to be able to adapt to a challenging environment. The appointment as a Prison Service Manager and the Graduate Trainee Manager Programme in Scotland are very similar in relation to the expectations, processes and competencies of the promotion and appointment processes of becoming a Prison Service Manager and National Offender Management Scheme in England and Wales. Please refer to the part of this chapter that discusses this for detailed information.

*P*rison Service Manager, 'The job of a Prison Service Manager is not what I thought it would be. It is more varied and definitely more stressful. I spend a lot of my time behind a desk but I always have to be responsive to what may be going on in the prison. '

The Prison Service in Northern Ireland

The structure of the Prison Service in Northern Ireland

The Northern Ireland Prison Service forms part of the Department of Justice. As an agency of the Justice Sector, the Northern

Ireland Prison Service works towards making the Justice System work in a more effective manner by concentrating on the vision as set out by the Justice Minister, David Ford (indirect, December 2013). As part of this vision the Northern Ireland Prison Service aims to improve public safety and reduce re-offending by managing and rehabilitating the offenders that are placed within its custody. The person with overall responsibility for the organisation is the Director General and at the time of writing this is Sue McAllister and the legislation that governs the practice within Northern Ireland is the Prison Act (Northern Ireland) 1953.

Action point

Find the Prison Act on the Northern Ireland Prison Service website. Make a note of the statutory duties of the Prison Service.

Reflection point

It is important to note when looking at the history of the Northern Ireland Prison Service that from 1969 30 staff members have been killed because of their association with the service and that many others, including family members, have been subjected to physical, emotional and verbal abuse and as such the organisation has held a crucial role with problems associated within Northern Ireland.

At the time of writing this text the Northern Ireland Prison Service has been subject to a process of reform informed by the *Strategic Efficiency and Effectiveness programme* (SEE). This reform process started in 2011 as a result of an interim report that stated that end-to-end changes needed to be made in relation to the whole of the Prison Service and estate. A number of previous reviews and inspection reports have also influenced this reform. The Strategic Efficiency and Effectiveness programme is intended to deliver results by 2015.

Intended results focus on the following:

- developing a motivated staff force that are well trained and professional;
- being well led;
- being cost-effective;
- maintaining the offender focus throughout;
- reducing offending and risk especially on release;
- improving relationships with the community it serves.

Action point

Download the Strategic Efficiency and Effectiveness programme documentation from the Department of Justice Northern Ireland website. Take time to read the document, noting down the key issues raised.

The Northern Ireland Prison Service within its documentation clearly state the vision, mission, purpose, aims and values of the work that it does and it is crucial that when looking towards a career in this service you are fully aware of these and how they will be linked to the recruitment and selection process.

It is important when looking at the system in Northern Ireland that you are aware of some key facts and figures.

Key facts and figures (Department of Justice Northern Ireland, December 2013):

- 2 adult prisons
- 1 young offenders centre
- around 1,800 people in custody
- 1,193 male sentenced prisoners
- 42 female sentenced prisoners
- 379 male unsentenced prisoners
- 17 female unsentenced prisoners

- 122 sentenced male young offenders
- 2 sentenced female young offenders
- 38 unsentenced male young offenders
- 3 unsentenced female young offenders
- 5 years represents the average sentence length
- 2,350 staff employed in the service.

Reflection point

What do these facts tell us? How do they differ from those in England and Wales and Scotland?

Working in the Northern Ireland Prison Service

The Northern Ireland Prison Service, in line with its mission statement, values a diverse staff group and as such encourages applications from people from all sectors of life, backgrounds and with a range of experiences. This is in line with England and Wales and Scotland. Applications are welcomed both from *graduates* and *non-graduates* alike and within this section of the chapter these will be highlighted where appropriate.

Working within the Northern Ireland Prison Service you would form part of the wider justice sector and you would also be responsible to the workings of the Civil Service. The Service has a clearly stated commitment to providing equality of opportunity and in ensuring that the staff force that is employed are valued, respected and representative of the communities that they serve. In relation to this *The Merit Principle* is applied, so that the best candidate is only recruited following a fair and transparent process.

*H*uman resources, 'It is each individual staff member's responsibility to understand the Equality of Opportunity policy and to work to it in practice.'

As part of the Strategic, Efficiency and Effectiveness programme recruitment processes within the Prison Service in Northern Ireland have been under review and following the Owers Review in 2011, fundamental changes have been made to the working practices of the Prison System especially in relation to deaths in custody. This has also placed different requirements on the staff that are employed.

Action point

Go onto the Northern Ireland Prisoner Ombudsman website and download the Owers Report 2011. What do the recommendations tell us about the changes that needed to be made within the system?

Write these recommendations down and think about their implications.

In 2012, as a result of the above, the Northern Ireland Prison Service launched its first recruitment campaign in 20 years. This campaign closed following recruitment to 200 new jobs. At the time of writing this book there were no current vacancies advertised.

Becoming a Custody Officer (Prison Officer) in Northern Ireland

Reflection point

At the time of writing this text the Custody Officer role is a relatively new one and replaces more traditionally the role of a Prison Officer.

Think about how this role may differ and the expectations that will be placed on you in this role.

The Custody Officer role is clearly defined in relation to the duties and responsibilities and these include (Insidetime Scotland, March 2014):

- provision of safe and secure custody;
- promotion of decent custody;
- prisoner engagement;
- general and administrative.

Eligibility criteria and entry requirements

In Northern Ireland recruitment to a Custody Officer post is carried out centrally. Vacancies are usually advertised on the Northern Ireland Prison Service website.

To be considered for a Custody Officer role you will need:

- to be willing to work in any of the prison establishments in Northern Ireland;
- to have a grade C or above (or equivalent) in English and maths;
- to be in good health;
- to be able to meet clearly stated fitness criteria;
- to have a current and clean driving licence;
- to be able to evidence good communication skills;
- to be able to work as part of a team;
- to be able to evidence problem-solving skills;
- to be able to act on your initiative;
- to deal with stressful and demanding situations;
- to be systematic;
- to be able to work with a range of people regardless of who they are.

Reflection point

Review what you read in Chapter 4 of this book. Pay particular attention to the skills described, particularly resilience.

All of the Northern Ireland Prison Service recruitment and selection practice for the role of a Custody Officer is based on a clearly defined competency framework.

As a Custody Officer you will be required to be able to commit to around a 40-hour week. As the Prison Service of Northern Ireland operates 24 hours a day and 365 days a year you will be required to work a shift pattern and be able to commit to working overtime, and according to the needs of the institution you work in at sometimes relatively short periods of notice. The starting salary at the time of writing is approximately £18,000 and you would be entitled to 25 days annual leave and 12 days public holiday.

Application process

The application process for the role of a Custody Officer has quite distinct and separate stages. These stages are similar to those within England and Wales and Scotland and involve numeracy and literacy tests, attendance at an Assessment Centre and an interview.

Please refer to the earlier exercises in the chapter relating to assessment centres, as they will assist you in your preparation.

Candidates will need to be successful at each stage of the process and will need to ensure that they pass the numeracy and literacy tests, as these form the basis of shortlisting for the next stages in the process and the Assessment Centre. These tests and the Assessment Centre are carried out by external organisations to the Northern Ireland Prison Service. If you are successful beyond the numeracy and literacy tests you will be sent full details in a pack with practice tests and exercises.

C*areers Advisor*, 'Evidence from students' participation in similar tests as part of an employability related module has shown that Criminal Justice students rate below the national graduate average for their maths ability. Practice makes perfect especially in relation to maths. GCSE Bitesize maths is a good resource to use.'

If you are successful in all of the stages of recruitment and are appointed, you will be required to obtain a Certificate of Competence. This is mandatory and will need to be achieved within 18–24 months following your appointment.

Becoming a Prison Service Manager in Northern Ireland

Within the Prison Service in Northern Ireland there are a range of opportunities for promotion to Senior Officer Grades and Governor Officer grades. Please refer to the sections on England and Wales and Scotland as the recruitment processes and competencies are similar to those already described.

Chapter summary

This chapter has hopefully encouraged you to start to think about what different roles are available in the Prison Services within the UK. Within the chapter there has been a discussion about the roles that are available and the particular recruitment and selection processes relating to the role of a Prison Officer and to that of a Prison Service Manager. Included throughout the chapter are action and reflection tasks that you will think about and complete. Finally some top tips from the chapter have been included. We hope that you have enjoyed reading the chapter and that you are more informed about what you will need to do to secure a job within this part of the sector should you choose to apply.

Top tips

- Think of your contribution to a team.
- How do you know you have communicated effectively?
- How do you make your degree relevant?
- What is the core focus of your dissertation/work-based learning project?
- How can you evidence your skills?
- Understand the organisation.
- Take time to read and familiarise yourself with the recruitment process.
- Give yourself time to complete the application form correctly.
- Practise your communication skills.
- Understand the assessment criteria.
- Know the difference between essential and desirable selection criteria.
- Practise your presentation skills, including your non-verbal communication.
- Be aware of your values and motivations.
- Think about why you want the job that you have applied for.

Some useful websites

- www.justice.gov.uk (The website of the Ministry of Justice)
- www.prisonreformtrust.org.uk (The website of the Prison Reform Trust)
- www.nationalarchives.gov.uk (The official website of the national archives of the government)
- www.sfjuk.com (The website of the sector skills council Skills for Justice)
- www.sps.gov.uk (The website of the Scottish Prison Service)
- www.shldirect.com (A test preparation and careers centre website)
- www.dojni.gov.uk (The website of the Northern Ireland Prison Service)
- www.howardleague.org (The website of the Howard League for Penal Reform)
- www.gov.uk/government/organisations/hm-prison-service (The website of the Prison Service)
- www.bbc.co.uk/bitesize/maths/ (The website for GCSE BiteSize Maths)
- www.niprisonerombudsman.com (The website of the Northern Ireland Ombudsman)

Recommended reading

Cavadino, M., Dignan, J. and Mair, G. (2013) *The Penal System. An introduction*. 5th edition. London: Sage

Coyle, A. (2005) *Understanding Prisons Key Issues in Policy and Practice*. Open University Press

Crawley, E. (2006) *Doing Prison Work*. Cullompton: Willan

Crewe, B. and Bennett, J. (2011) *The Prisoner*. Abingdon: Routledge

Jewkes, Y. and Bennett, J. (Eds) (2008) *Dictionary of Prisons and Punishment*. Cullompton: Willan

Liebling, A., Price, D. and Shefer, G. (2011) *The Prison Officer*. Cullompton: Willan

Logan, C.H. (1990) *Private Prisons: Pros and cons*. Oxford: Oxford University Press

References

Bromley Briefings Prison factfile (2013) Retrieved from www.prison reformtrust.org.uk/publications/factfile (accessed 27 May 2014)

Ministry of Justice (2014, January) HM prison service: public sector prisons. Retrieved from www.gov.uk/government/organisations/hm-prison-service

Scottish Prison Service (2014) Retrieved from www.sps.gov.uk (accessed 27 May 2014)

chapter 8

Working in the Courts, Prosecution Services and advocacy

Chapter objectives

By the end of this chapter you should be able to:

■ understand the structure of the Courts in England and Wales, Scotland and Northern Ireland;

■ understand the structure of the Prosecution Services in England and Wales, Scotland and Northern Ireland;

■ identify the range of roles available within the Courts and prosecution sector;

■ understand the routes to becoming a solicitor;

■ understand the routes to becoming a barrister.

Introduction to the Courts, Prosecution Services and advocacy

When looking at the agencies in the Criminal Justice System it is perhaps the Court System that most is known about. The workings and practice of the Courts are there for all to see, and images about their role, function and effectiveness are a constant cause for debate. The Courts, Prosecution Services and the process of advocacy are an integral part of the Criminal Justice Process and society, and the Courts are the places where justice is seen to be done. If you have ever sat in a courtroom or watched a court-based drama on the television, what you are witnessing is the result of a long legal evolutionary process and the result of a series of stages that occur from the point that someone is arrested to the point that they actually appear in court. These stages involve a decision to prosecute based on the evidence that the Police have gathered and the nature of the case that will be taken forward to the courts.

Reflection point

It is important to note that nearly all of the main agencies and structures discussed in this text are involved in the practice and procedure of the Courts and Prosecution Services and as such serve as a good example of the multidisciplinary nature of the work of the Criminal Justice sector.

The Courts, Prosecution Services and advocacy offer a variety of different roles for graduates and non-graduates alike as well as a range of promotional opportunities for career development. Some of these roles include positions as a Paralegal, an Usher, a Legal Researcher, a Court Clerk, a Court Manager, a solicitor, a barrister and of course a judge. Due to the variety of roles within this sector it is our intention to discuss the roles of a *Court Manager*, a *Court Clerk*, a *Crown Prosecutor* and a *Crown Advocate*. We have selected these specific roles/careers as they provide the reader with insight into the work of the Courts, prosecution and advocacy services and the natural career progression through the services and because of the feedback received from students currently studying on related degree programmes. The entry requirements and application process will be considered for each role before moving through to a more general analysis of the skills needed to be successful in securing employment within this part of the Criminal Justice System. In discussing these roles we will be separating the chapter into two distinct sections; the Courts and the Prosecution Service. The role of advocacy will run through both of the sections. Where appropriate there will be a general discussion of the routes to becoming a qualified *solicitor* or *barrister* as these apply to the qualified legal roles in both areas.

Action point

When you are considering your career choices in the Courts and Prosecution Service you would benefit from completing some voluntary work experience in the Criminal Justice sector, although not essential it is desirable and would place you at an advantage when identifying and demonstrating skills and competencies.

Within the UK there is not one single unified system and as such it is important that you pay attention to the differences between the jurisdictions of England and Wales, Scotland and Northern Ireland. Within this chapter there will be a separate discussion about the recruitment processes and practice in the different jurisdictions, although the similarities will be noted where they apply. It is important that you consider these differences and the implications of them for the area and role that you wish to apply to and work in.

Having reviewed Chapter 2 of this text and read the suggested texts you will have a broad understanding of the role of the Courts and Prosecution Services within the broader Criminal Justice System so it is the intention of this chapter to build on this knowledge by providing a *brief overview* of the Court and Prosecution System and in doing so explore the *key principles* that underpin it. This is important because only by understanding these principles will you be able to place in context what the Courts and Prosecution Services actually do and understand the role that they play within the broader Criminal Justice System. *Key figures* will be provided as an integral part of the chapter in relation to the number of courts, the number of cases processed through them and the number of people working within the system. The chapter will then move on to consider the different roles and career options available within the system and, as an integral part of this, explore the skills and competencies required when working within this sector.

It is intended that this chapter will give you the opportunity to give informed consideration to the actual workings of the system by providing practical advice and guidance from those currently working within the system. We hope that this will provide you with a realistic presentation of a range of activities that you could be involved in and highlight the importance of the practice, skills and knowledge required to carry out the role you are considering.

Action point

Have a look at the different Courts and Prosecution Service websites for England and Wales, Scotland and Northern Ireland and write down the key differences in the work that they do and the roles that are available.

The Criminal Courts

This section of the chapter will provide an overview of the Criminal Courts within the UK. In doing this the structure and function of the Criminal Courts in England and Wales, Scotland and Northern Ireland will first be discussed and the chapter will then move on to looking at working in this part of the Criminal Justice System. Throughout the discussion you will see similarities between the processes and practice, with each court system having a clearly defined hierarchical structure.

The Criminal Courts in England and Wales

Within England and Wales, HM Courts and Tribunals Service govern the criminal, civil and family courts and the tribunal work and administration of the courts. This service works as an agency of the Ministry of Justice and was formed in 2011, bringing together two previously separate agencies, those of the Courts and the tribunal services. The agency is accountable to a board with an independent chair; it is the chairs responsibility to ensure that the agency delivers the aims and objectives as set out below. Within its approximate 650 different locations the agency employs around 20,000 staff and handles over 2 million criminal cases, 150,000 family disputes and 1.8 civil matters (Justice.gov 2013).

Action point

Have a look at the Ministry of Justice website and locate the statistics relevant to the Courts. What do these statistics tell us about who appears in court and the nature of the cases that are dealt with?

It is important to note here that while Scotland and Northern Ireland have a separate court system the work of HM Courts and Tribunal Service also deals with non-devolved tribunals in these areas. These are tribunal matters that are reserved to the parliament at Westminster.

The Criminal Courts deal with the cases that are brought as a result of a criminal prosecution. Within the Criminal Court structure there is a clearly defined hierarchy. The lower courts, such as the magistrates' courts hear the less serious, 'summary' cases with the more serious, 'indictable' matters being heard in the Crown Court. There is also a route of appeal through the court structure.

> **Action point**
>
> If you do not understand the terms 'summary' and 'indictable' take time to research them. An understanding of these two terms will assist you in understanding how criminal cases are dealt with and processed through the courts.

> **Action point**
>
> Have a look at the gov.uk website and read the information that describes the working of the court in more detail.

The magistrates' court

The magistrates' court can be described as the workhorse of the court system, as all criminal cases regardless of their seriousness start in it. The magistrates' court also deals with around 95 per cent of all criminal cases, dealing with both fact and law (Sanders and Young 2010). Magistrates therefore decide on guilt/innocence and the sentence to be imposed. This is an important difference from the Crown Court where it is a jury that decides on guilt/innocence and the judge that imposes the sentence. The magistrates' court has limited sentencing powers and in relation to the imposition of a prison sentence can only sentence someone to a maximum of 6 months' custody for a single offence increasing to 12 months where multiple offences are being dealt with. Magistrates also sit in Youth Courts and are involved in civil work.

In most cases within a magistrates' court, magistrates sit in panels of three. Where possible there is an attempt to ensure a representative mix of people on the panel but in reality this is not always possible. A Court Clerk assists the panel of magistrates in the role that they have. This role will be discussed later in the chapter.

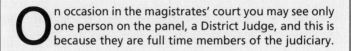

On occasion in the magistrates' court you may see only one person on the panel, a District Judge, and this is because they are full time members of the judiciary.

The Crown Court

The Crown Court deals with the more serious of criminal cases and/or cases that have been referred from the magistrates' court. The Crown Court acts both as a sentencing court and an appeal court for the decisions reached in the magistrates' court. There are different types of Crown Courts that sit across England and Wales with the distinction being made according to the type of work that the court deals with. This is usually linked to the seriousness of the offences. A judge hears cases in the Crown Court, the role of the judge is mainly to oversee and manage the court process, and to pass sentence. The judge does not have the power to decide upon guilt, this is the role of the jury. In deciding upon guilt the jury is not required to justify the decision made, just simply to state it in open court. The jury in England and Wales is composed of 12 randomly selected people; its intention is to bring the 'ordinary' person into the court process. The jury has two possible verdicts, that of guilty or not guilty.

Reflection point

Lay magistrates make decisions within the magistrates' courts while in the Crown Courts the same decisions are made by a judge and a jury.

Consider some of the implications of this and how it may impact on the role that you have.

The Criminal Courts in Scotland

The Scottish Court Service is the body that is responsible for the management and operation of the courts within Scotland. The

Scottish Court Service is governed by a board of people and is chaired by the Lord President. The Lord President is the most senior judge in Scotland. In Scotland cases are referred as either solemn cases or summary cases. Solemn cases are those more serious cases and are dealt with in the highest court and summary cases being of a less serious nature are dealt with in the lower courts. This is similar to the process in England and Wales and Northern Ireland. In Scotland there is a three-tier criminal court structure: the High Court, the Sheriff Court and Justice of the Peace Courts. All of these courts hear criminal cases and decide both on guilt and sentence. In Scotland there are three different types of verdict available to the courts. These are guilty, not guilty and not proven.

Action point

The Scottish Court's website is a useful source of information on the courts. Go onto the website and familiarise yourself with the information it provides about the different courts that operate in Scotland.

The High Court

The High Court is Scotland's most senior court and, similar to the crown court, it deals with the most serious of criminal cases 'solemn' cases. The High Court has three permanent bases in Scotland: in Edinburgh, Glasgow and Aberdeen. The High Court also sits in other cities and towns in Scotland but this is on a periodic and not permanent basis. The jurisdiction of the High Court covers the whole of Scotland. Within The High Court it is a judge and a jury that decides upon law and fact. The role of the judge and jury is similar to that in England and Wales.

courts, prosecution services and advocacy

A jury in Scotland is made up of 15 people. This differs from both England and Wales and Northern Ireland where it is 12. A majority of 8 to 7 is needed for a person to be found guilty.

The Sheriff Court

The Sheriff Court deals with the majority of criminal and civil court cases in Scotland. At the time of writing there are 142 sheriffs that sit in 49 different courtrooms. The Sheriff Court can deal with both solemn and summary cases and so the sheriffs that preside over the court have to have knowledge of every aspect of the law. Similar to that of the magistrates' court the Sheriff Court can be viewed as the workhorse of the system in Scotland, as they deal with the majority of cases that are processed through the system. The only exception to this are those crimes reserved to the High Court.

Reflection point

The role of a Sheriff is similar to that of a judge. A jury can also sit for solemn cases in the Sheriff Court.

The criminal jurisdiction of the Sheriff Court is therefore both summary and solemn. The type of case that is being heard dictates the sentencing powers. The Queen, based on recommendations made by the First Minister, appoints Sheriffs. These appointments can only be made when someone has been qualified as an advocate or solicitor for a minimum of ten years.

Justice of the Peace Courts

A Justice of the Peace Court is similar to a magistrates' court in England and Wales in that it is a layperson, a magistrate, that presides over the court. Justice of the Peace Courts are relatively new in the court process, replacing District Courts in 2007 they deal with the least serious of offences such as those concerned with speeding and are located locally, dealing with cases specific to that area. In most cases within a Justice of the Peace Court, magistrates sit in panels of three. Where possible there is an attempt to ensure a representative mix of people on the panel but in reality this is not always possible.

The Criminal Courts in Northern Ireland

The Northern Ireland Courts and Tribunal Service is the body responsible for the administrative support for the court system, both criminal and civil, and for the support of an independent judiciary.

Reflection point

The Criminal Courts system in Northern Ireland is similar to that in England and Wales in that the main courts are magistrate's and Crown Court. Please refer to the section on England and Wales and Chapter 2 of this text for information regarding these courts and their operation.

Working in the Courts Service

As previously stated in the chapter there are a variety of interesting roles that you could apply for within the Courts Service in the UK. This section of the chapter will provide an overview of some of those roles including the role of a Court Manager and a Court Clerk. Within each of these roles there is a clearly defined internal progression pathway.

Most vacancies within this sector are advertised via the Ministry of Justice, the Scottish Court Service and the Northern Ireland Court Service. Employment within this sector is covered by the Skills for Justice sector Skills Council.

Action point

Think about the above roles. What do you think they involve? When you have done this have a look at the relevant websites for England and Wales and Scotland and note down the key points to consider for each role that is described.

To improve your employability try to gain some work experience in a court.

Court Manager

As a Court Manager you would be responsible for the efficient and effective day-to-day management of the court process and the people within it. A primary role within this is also to serve the public. Each court or set of courts has a Court Manager. The role will include people management, the allocation of resources, liaising with a wide range of people, ensuring that legislation and policy is adhered to and the management of budgets. Within this the following skills are seen to be essential:

- communication skills
- customer service skills
- strong organisational skills
- excellent presentation skills
- technical skills
- diagnostic skills.

The role of a Court Manager is open to graduates and non-graduates. All applications are processed through the relevant courts service for the area you wish to work in. If you are considering this role as a graduate, a relevant degree such as Criminal Justice or Law would be beneficial. If you are a non-graduate you can apply after you have completed your school education, although minimum GCSE results will be needed. To progress to a Court Manager role straight from school you would most probably start in a case administrator role. A further entry option is via the completion of a Business and Administration apprenticeship or a Courts, Tribunals and Prosecution Operations apprenticeship.

As a Court Manager you will earn in the region of £19,000–£30,000, although this may depend on the size of the court that you manage. The application process will require you to complete a competency based application form and attend for an interview. You may also be required to submit a CV.

Court Clerk

A Court Clerk is a legally qualified solicitor or barrister. (Please refer to the general discussion later in this chapter on becoming a qualified solicitor.)

A Court Clerk works as an officer of the court and is employed by the relevant governing body of the courts. In Scotland they may be known as the 'clerk of the court' or 'clerk of the peace'. The main role of the Court Clerk is to assist the legal processes and advise the magistrates or Justices of the Peace sitting in the relevant court, however there are other areas of work that you will be required to do.

Role of a Court Clerk:

- to keep up-to-date with the law;
- to assist magistrates and guide on points of law;
- to make sure that all relevant papers are prepared in time for the court case;
- to complete the paperwork that magistrates order;
- to deal with legal aid applications;
- to train magistrates and legal advisors.

As a Court Clerk you will start on a salary of between £18,000 and £30,000. This will be dependent on the court that you are working in. This salary will progress the more experienced you are to between £40,000 and £50,000. As a Court Clerk there is a clearly defined promotion route from a tier one and you can progress until you reach the equivalent of a tier five. As a qualified solicitor or barrister you will have completed the training and qualification process, however Court Clerks need to also complete a training programme designed to cover the work that you will be required to do. Throughout this training programme you will be supported by an experienced Court Clerk. The application process will require you to complete a competency based application form and attend an interview. You may also be required to submit a CV.

Action point

Read Chapter 4 of this text and think about what you will need to demonstrate at each stage of the application process. Refer also to websites such as Prospects for additional information.

Reflection point

The role of a magistrate or Justice of the Peace is a crucial role within the courts. This is a voluntary role. You can become a magistrate from the age of 18 and need no formal qualifications. You will, however, have to demonstrate through a rigorous process that you have the necessary skills to become a magistrate. These skills include an awareness of social issues, responsibility, organisation and the ability to communicate properly. The Ministry of Justice website has further information regarding the role and the application process.

The Prosecution Service

This section of the chapter will provide an overview of the Prosecution Services within the UK. We will start with a general discussion of the role of the Prosecution Service and the basis upon which prosecution decisions are made. We will then look at the Prosecution Services in England and Wales, Scotland and Northern Ireland before moving on to looking at working in this part of the Criminal Justice System.

Once a crime has been committed and investigated by the Police, a decision is made based on the facts and evidence of the case on whether a case should proceed to be prosecuted in the criminal courts or whether another course of action such as a diversionary measure should be the result. It is important to note that if the evidence is not sufficient then no action could also be the result. Within the UK it is the Prosecution Services that make the decision. The Prosecution Services in the UK are seperate and independent from the Police.

In considering whether a case should proceed to the courts, the Prosecution Services need to consider applying two separate tests. These are the Evidential Test and the Public Interest Test.

Reflection point

The Evidential Test requires the Prosecution Services to look at whether the evidence is sufficient, reliable and admissible. If this test is not made then the case should be referred back to the Police or stopped. The Public Interest Test follows the Evidential Test and here the Prosecution Services need to give consideration to issues to do with the seriousness of the offence, the length of time since the offence was committed and any other relevant factors.

It is important to familiarise yourself with the relevant websites of the Prosecution Service you are looking to work within.

The Prosecution Service in England and Wales

The Crown Prosecution Service is the agency in England and Wales that is responsible for the prosecution and presentation of criminal cases on behalf of the state. Within this it also reviews and advises the Police on cases to be taken forward to the courts for prosecution. The Crown Prosecution Service was established in 1986 following the Prosecution of Offences Act 1985. This piece of legislation established the Director of Public Prosecutions.

Reflection point

Initially the Crown Prosecution Service's main focus was to take over the responsibility of a case from the Police once an individual had been charged. This remained the situation until the Criminal Justice Act 2003 extended the powers that the Crown Prosecution Service have, enabling them to charge suspects rather than the Police. Consider the implications of this change for the work of the Crown Prosecution Service and their relationship with the Police.

The Crown Prosecution Service has no investigatory powers and as such the agency relies on the work of the Police and the way in which they have investigated a case. The Crown Prosecution Service, in deciding which cases go to court, uses two separate tests. The first is The Evidential Test and the second is The Public Interest Test.

Action point

What factors do you think the Crown Prosecution Service should take into account when deciding to prosecute a case and take it forward to the court?
Does this differ from what is actually taken into account?

The Crown Prosecution Service clearly lays out the mission and values that underpin the work that it does within two key documents, *the Core Quality Standards* and *the Code for Crown Prosecutors*. When you are looking at a career in this sector it is important that you are aware of how these may impact on the work that you do.

Our aims

- to protect the public
- to support victims and witnesses
- to ensure that justice is achieved.

Action point

Go onto the Crown Prosecution Service website and download the Core Quality Standards and Code for Crown Prosecutors documents.

Our mission

To deliver justice through the independent and effective prosecution of crime, fostering a culture of excellence by supporting and inspiring each other to be the best that we can.

Our values

- to be independent and fair
- to be honest and open
- to treat every individual with respect
- to behave professionally
- to strive for excellence.

It is important when considering a career in this sector that you are aware of some key facts and figures.

Key facts

- 13 geographical areas
- 4 specialist casework divisions
- 6,840 people employed by the CPS nationally
- 2,350 prosecutors
- 4,110 caseworkers and administrators
- 93 per cent of the workforce employed in frontline prosecution activities.

The Prosecution Service in Scotland

The Crown Office and Procurator Fiscal Service (COPFS) is Scotland's Prosecution Service and is responsible for the prosecution of criminal behaviour in Scotland. This office covers the whole of Scotland and is seen as having an essential role in the overall aim of the justice sector in making Scotland a safer place to live. The Crown and Procurator Fiscal Service is a department of the Scottish Government and is headed by the Lord Advocate. The options that are available to the Prosecution Services in Scotland are outlined in the Crown Office and Procurator Fiscal Service Code 2005. The work of the Crown Office and Procurator Fiscal Service is similar in nature to that of the Crown Prosecution Service in England and Wales and Northern Ireland.

The Crown Office and Procurator Fiscal Service clearly lay out the mission and values that underpin the work that it does (COPFS 2014). When you are looking at a career in this sector it is important that you are aware of how these may impact on the work that you do.

Our values

to be professional;
to show respect.

Our priorities

to reduce crime, especially hate crime;
to support victims;
to increase public confidence.

Our roles and responsibilities

to investigate, prosecute and disrupt crime;
to establish the cause of sudden and unexpected deaths;
to investigate allegations of criminal conduct against the Police.

Our objectives

to secure the confidence of the community;
to prioritise the prosecution of serious crime;
to ensure that all deaths are reported to the Procurator Fiscal.

The Prosecution Service in Northern Ireland

In Northern Ireland it is the Public Prosecution Service (PPS) that is responsible for the prosecution of criminal behaviour. The Public Prosecution Service was established in 2005 following the Justice Act (NI) 2002. The Director of Public Prosecutions for Northern Ireland heads the Public Prosecution Service. The Public Prosecution Service carries out similar functions to the Crown Prosecution Service in England and Wales however it is organised differently. The work of the Public Prosecution Service is governed by the Code for Prosecutors Revised 2008. All of the staff employed by the service are classed as civil servants.

Action point

Go onto the Public Prosecution Service website and download the Code for Prosecutors.

The Public Prosecution Service clearly states on its website that its intention is to work closely with the other areas of the Criminal Justice System in order to protect the people and community of Northern Ireland.

Our vision

to be recognised as providing a first class Prosecution Service.

Our aim

to provide the people of NI with an independent and impartial assessment of the evidence and the public interest.

Our values

to be independent and impartial;
to have a shared purpose;
to be excellent;
to communicate openly and honestly;
to work in partnership with other agencies and organisations.

Reflection point

Think about how your values may or may not fit in with those outlined by the service. Remember, values are individual and personal commitments to what you believe to be morally right and you need to understand what it is you believe in and what you believe to be right courses of action.

The work that both the Prosecution Services do in Scotland and Northern Ireland and the decisions they make are the same as in England and Wales.

Working in the Prosecution Service

As previously stated in the chapter there are a variety of interesting roles that you could apply for within the Prosecution Service in the UK. This section of the chapter will provide an overview of some of the roles available within the organisation. The Prosecution Service separates the roles that are available into three broadly defined categories, these are legal careers, professional careers and apprenticeships. Within this part of the chapter it is the intention of the authors to focus on the legal careers section.

Reflection point

Think about these three different areas and note the roles available within them. There are opportunities within the areas of professional careers and apprenticeships that you may not have considered such as a Diversity Officer.

The Prosecution Services advertise their vacancies via the relevant website or Civil Service jobs website. Full details of the application process are provided with the individual job advert, however all of the application processes are competency based and so the application form that you complete will need to evidence the criteria clearly laid out in the person specification for each role. Employment within this sector is covered by the Skills for Justice Sector Skills Council.

Legal careers

In order to work in the Prosecution Service in this capacity you will need to be either a *qualified solicitor*, *barrister* or *have started your legal training*. Within the Crown Prosecution Service for example there is also a *Legal Training Scheme*. This was launched in 2012 and offers those wishing to work within the Crown Prosecution Service the opportunity to complete their legal training by offering pupilages and/or training contracts.

As a legally qualified practitioner within the Crown Prosecution Service there are a number of different roles that you can be employed in. The roles of Crown Prosecutor/Procurator Fiscal/Public Prosecutar and Crown Advocate will now be discussed.

Crown Prosecutors/Procurator Fiscal/Public Prosecutor

Crown Prosecutors hold a key role in the work of the Crown Prosecution Service. The role will require you to be involved in the following activities: the review of cases investigated by the Police, the prosecution of cases in court and the giving of advice to a range of organisations especially the Police during the prosecution process. The role is therefore varied and challenging. Within this role there is a clearly defined career progression structure through to a Senior Crown Prosecutor and indeed promotion and progression can also start with your work as a case administrator.

> *C*rown Prosecutor, 'I never thought that I would be able to be promoted in the way that I have been. I entered as a non-graduate and now I am working in a legal capacity as a qualified solicitor.'

Within the recruitment documentation it is clearly stated that the skills that you will need to be able to demonstrate and evidence are:

- advocacy skills
- organisational skills
- team working skills
- working under pressure
- responding effectively to challenges
- personal judgement skills
- accuracy skills.

Action point

Look at the skills listed above. It is important that you think about these and importantly how you will evidence them.

Crown Advocate/Advocate Deputies/Senior Public Prosecutor

The role of a Crown Advocate is integral to the work of the Prosecution Service. The role is primarily aimed at offering a level of consistency in relation to the work it does with victims and witnesses and to the overall operations of the court. The Prosecution Service places an emphasis on the Crown Advocate acquiring expertise in particular areas of work such as gun crime, rape and serious violence cases. For example, in an attempt to ensure this expertise, in 2012 the Crown Prosecution Service established Complex Crime Divisions in the areas of counter terrorism, organised crime and Special Crime Divisions.

Having considered some of the different roles available, this chapter will now move on to looking at the routes to becoming a solicitor and barrister as they apply to some of the roles above.

Becoming a solicitor

Solicitors primarily offer legal advice on a range of issues from every-day issues, to protecting people's rights, to supporting the local community. You could also be based in a variety of work situations: in private businesses, in private practice, in local or national government. Solicitors can also work in both a criminal and civil capacity. As a mature student or someone looking for a change of career, becoming a solicitor could be exactly what you are looking for as applications are welcomed from mature students and those looking for a change in career focus.

Action point

Download the guide to becoming a solicitor as a mature student and career changer from the Law Society website.

Reflection point

Qualifying as a solicitor is both a long and costly process and this may vary depending on when you decide to become a solicitor and on whether your degree is a qualifying Law degree.

The Law Society serves as the representative body for all solicitors in England and Wales and offers a range of services and useful resources to support the work that solicitors do. Both Scotland and Northern Ireland have equivalent representative bodies.

Familiarise yourself with the Law Society website and the equivalent websites in Scotland and Northern Ireland.

Salary ranges for qualified solicitors are around £18,000 for starting as a solicitor and between £25,000 and £75,000 for more experienced solicitors. This can increase up to £100,000 for partners in large firms. As a solicitor you can expect to work long hours and this will include weekends. The work that you will do will be largely office based although some travel may be required depending upon the work that you are doing and the people you are representing.

Reflection point

Consider the implications this may have on your lifestyle. Would working long and sometimes unsociable hours suit you?

Practising Solicitor, 'Considerable commitment is needed not only to qualify as a solicitor but also to work as one. It is important to research the career fully and look at the expectations.'

Key skills needed to become a solicitor

- dedication
- professionalism
- a sense of responsibility
- commercial awareness

- numeracy skills
- time management skills
- ability to prioritise
- ability to understand situations
- communication skills
- IT skills.

*S*olicitor, 'Important to match your skills with what is required form you. A key skill that I use every day is my ability to understand situations and the problems that I may be faced with.'

There are many routes within England and Wales that lead you to qualifying and working as a solicitor. Within this part of the chapter the routes discussed will be the traditional route via higher education and the Chartered Legal Executive Lawyers (CILEx) route.

The traditional route to becoming a solicitor

This route is a graduate entry route.
Taking a qualifying Law degree is the easiest route to becoming a solicitor, but this clearly depends upon you knowing what it is that you want to do.

Action point

If you are certain that being a solicitor is the career for you then you should check the Law Society website for full information regarding the qualifying Law degrees.

If you are considering a change of career or hold a non-qualifying degree you will need to do either a *Common Professional*

Examination (CPE) or a *Graduate Diploma in Law* (GDL). These are both mandatory qualifications.

Reflection point

Cost is an important factor here. Fees can vary at the time of writing between £3,000 and £9,000 for a year for these courses. Can you commit to this cost?

Prior to becoming a solicitor you must undertake a period of vocational training. This is known as a *Legal Practice Course* (LPC). This can be studied either on a 1-year full-time programme or a 2-year part-time programme. Again it is important to consider the cost implication as this part of the training programme at the time of writing is between £8,000 and £12,000.

The final stage in qualifying as a solicitor requires you to secure a *Training Contract*. Training contract vacancies are usually advertised in the Training Contract and Pupilage Handbook and the Chambers Student Guide. There are however a range of websites that also advertise training contract vacancies.

Action point

Bookmark and check websites such as lawcareers.net, prospects.ac.uk and lawgazette.co.uk for training contract vacancies. You may also want to check the organisations that you are interested in for information regarding their recruitment processes.

As part of the Training Contract you will be required to pass a *Professional Skills Course* (PCS). This requires you to attend a taught programme for 12 days. This course builds on the areas studied in the Legal Practitioners Course and is made up of a mixture of core modules and elective modules. It is important to note here that you need to be prepared to embark on a journey of continual professional development. Finally when you have completed all of these stages you can apply to become part of the roll of solicitors. Being successful and reaching this stage requires you to be determined, competitive, focussed and above all aware of the skills that you need for the sector you are going to apply for.

Chartered Legal Executive Lawyers Route (CILEx)

This route can be via either graduate or non-graduate entry and only exists in England and Wales. If you enter as a graduate you may be entitled to some credits for what you have already studied.

As a student on a Chartered Legal Executive Lawyers programme you could expect to earn between £15,000 and £28,000 per year and you will be required to study and pass two separate examinations. In addition you will need to also work in a legal capacity and have been supervised by a qualified solicitor. This can be up to a period of five years. If you are studying on a part time basis it can take you up to five years to qualify and pass the exams.

Action point

Go onto the CILEx website and look at the entry requirements, tests and conditions of service. If you do not meet these criteria what do you need to do to be eligible?

The Chartered Legal Lawyers Route also offers a route to graduates with a qualifying law degree and again full information regarding this can be found on the website.

Becoming a barrister

Barristers provide specialist legal advice and represent their clients in court. The role of a barrister is specifically to represent their clients in a court setting by translating the case or requirements into legal language. Barristers by the nature of the work that they do are duty bound to administer justice and so their role is crucial in the court process.

The Bar Council, for example, serves as the representative body of barristers in England and Wales. Its role is to support the profession and promote (The Bar Council 2013):

- the Bar's high quality specialist advocacy and advisory services;
- fair access to justice for all;
- the highest standards of ethics, equality and diversity;
- the development of business opportunities for barristers.

*B*arrister, 'Try and observe the work that a barrister does or watch films about the role.'

Working as a barrister can prove to be both a rewarding and challenging career. Qualified barristers can earn between £25,000 and £300,000 and can, after 10 years, reach £1,000,000. The salary that you receive can depend upon where you work, your experience, your expertise and your reputation. The hours that you do will vary, but will be mainly office hours from a Monday to Friday. You may be based in a court setting or in an office near to a court.

Reflection point

The Bar Council estimates that about 80 per cent of barristers are self-employed with most working in chambers linked to a law firm. If you were to secure a permanent position it would be referred to as a tenancy.

Training to become a barrister can offer both a rewarding and exciting career. In order to qualify as a barrister you will be required to complete three different stages of training: the academic stage, the vocational stage and a pupilage. At each of these different stages you will be required to demonstrate the skills required to 'act' as a barrister and advocate. The cost of becoming a barrister is similar to that of becoming a solicitor. It is important that you think about the implications of not only the time needed to qualify but the financial cost involved.

Key skills needed to become a barrister

- intellectual ability
- good command of written English
- good command of spoken English
- an ability to think and communicate under pressure
- determination
- stamina
- flexibility.

Reflection point

As with any other sector, the importance of gaining some work experience can not be underestimated. These opportunities in a law field could include gaining some experience in a solicitors or law firm, a mini-pupilage, pro-bono work and marshalling a judge. Experiences that you gain in a non-related law field are also important.

Chapter summary

This chapter has hopefully encouraged you to start to think about what different roles are available in the Courts, Prosecution and advocacy Services within the UK and how these services operate within England and Wales, Scotland and Northern Ireland. Within the chapter there has been a discussion about the roles that are available and the particular recruitment and selection processes that you will need to go through. Included throughout the chapter are action and reflection tasks that you will think about and complete. Finally some top tips from the chapter have been included. We hope that you have enjoyed reading the chapter and that you are more informed about what you will need to do to secure a job within this part of the sector should you choose to apply.

Top tips

- It is important to understand the sector.
- Understand the difference between the Courts and Prosecution Services.
- Take time to research the differences that exist between England and Wales, Northern Ireland and Scotland.
- Think about how you can evidence the skills needed.

- Understand what the recruitment and selection process requires from you; what are the different stages?
- If you know you want to be a solicitor or barrister then choose a qualifying Law degree.
- Think about the cost implications of becoming a solicitor or barrister.
- Get some work experience.
- Go and sit in the courts and watch what happens.
- Practise your presentation skills, including your non-verbal communication.
- Be aware of your values and motivations.
- Think about why you want the job that you have applied for.
- Use the career service at your school, college or university.

Some useful websites

- www.justice.gov.uk (Website of the Ministry of Justice)
- www.ppsni.gov.uk (Website of the Prosecution Services in Northern Ireland)
- www.sfjuk.com (Website of the sector skills council Skills for Justice)
- www.scottish.parliament.uk/ResearchBriefingsAndFactsheets/S4/SB_11–59.pdf (Information regarding the role of the Prosecution Service in Scotland)
- www.copfs.gov.uk (Website for the Prosecution Service in Scotland)
- www.scotland-judiciary.org.uk (Website for the Judiciary of Scotland)
- www.scotcourts.gov (Website for the Scottish Courts Service)
- www.dojni.gov.uk (Website for the Northern Ireland Criminal Justice System)
- www.judiciary.gov.uk (Website for the Judiciary in England and Wales)
- www.courtsni.gov.uk (Website for the Courts and Tribunal Service in Northern Ireland)
- www.lawsociety.org.uk (Website for the Solicitors Representative body in England and Wales)

- www.lawscot.org.uk (Website for the Solicitors Representative body in Scotland)
- www.lawsoc-ni.org.uk (Website for the Solicitors Representative body in Northern Ireland)
- www.barcouncil.org.uk (Website for barristers)
- www.nationalcareersservice.direct.gov.uk/Pages/Home.aspx (Careers information and advice for all)
- www.prospects.ac.uk (Careers information and advice website for graduate employability)
- www.cilex.org.uk (Website for CILEx)

Recommended reading

There is a wealth of sources that you could refer to in this section. Most Criminal Justice books will contain information on both the courts Services and Prosecution Services, as will the career information guides available. By researching the above websites and the other chapters in this text you will be able to locate the most useful to you.

References

Sanders, A. and Young, R. (2010) *Criminal Justice*. 4th edition. Oxford: Oxford University Press

COPFS (2014) Retrieved from www.copfs.gov.uk (accessed 27 May 2014)

Working in youth justice

Introduction to the Youth Offending Service

The Youth Offending Service is an integral part of the Criminal Justice System that deals with young people who are at risk of committing offences or who have become involved in offending behaviour. If you have an interest in working with and supporting change in young people then you should give serious consideration to a career within the Youth Offending Teams that are based in the community. These are *multi-agency* teams and will offer you plenty of variety to begin developing your skills and career structure. There are *in-service training* opportunities and, if you chose to, you could do further study and develop your career up the management structure.

Having read Chapter 2 of this text you will have begun to develop some understanding of how the services work together in the Criminal Justice System. This chapter will begin to introduce you to the Youth Offending Teams. It will begin by providing a brief overview of the development of the Youth Service in England and Wales. Governed by the Youth Justice Board, it is important to understand the *aims* and *objectives* that drive effective practice. This chapter will then move on to consider the functions and the structure of the Youth Offending Teams. The careers discussed are the *Youth Offending Team Officer*, the *Qualified Senior Practitioner/Case Manager* and then the *Team Manager*. These have been chosen to demonstrate the natural progression in the service. Practical guidance will be offered in the form of reflection and action points and comments from practitioners in the field will provide some insight into the skills and roles. The chapter will also give consideration to the Youth Justice Service in Northern Ireland and Scotland. Given the similarities in the roles and functions of the practitioners, we will not duplicate the material but discuss areas of difference.

Reflection point

There is variation in the use of the term *Young offenders*.

- In England and Wales Youth Offending Teams, the term is used to refer to those under the age of 18 and over the age of 10.
- In Scotland it is used for those aged 16–17.
- In Northern Ireland they do not use the term, only for those in custody.
- In the UK prison estate it is used for those 18–21.
- To those in the Probation Service (and other adult teams) it is used to refer to those 18–21.

working in youth justice

You also need to be familiar with the *age of responsibility.*

- England and Wales – 10
- Scotland – 8, however the age of criminal prosecution is 12
- Northern Ireland – 10

Action point

Thinking of the term *young offender*. What are your views on the age of responsibility? And on the use of the label?
   Look in the media and note headlines that involve young people. What do they say?

General overview of the Youth Offending Teams in England and Wales

The Youth Offending Teams were introduced by the *Crime and Disorder Act 1998* and they are multi-agency teams comprising members from both the statutory and voluntary organisations. They are managed by the local authority and overseen and guided by the Youth Justice Board. It is important to have some understanding of the historical context of the development of services for young people who offend.

Reflection point

The history of the treatment of young people in both society and the Criminal Justice System is an interesting one and this chapter will not be able to do it justice. For more in-depth reading we would suggest you read the texts written by academics such as John Muncie (2009).

Historically the development of the Youth Justice System can be explained as being caught up in an ongoing debate of *justice versus welfare and control*. We can see that early notions of young people were embroiled in the ideology of a class system; those of poorer backgrounds were seen as coming from the unruly class and as a consequence education was seen as a form of social control, but for those from more affluent backgrounds education was viewed as a necessity. The dominating view of the 1900s saw deviant behaviour as an individual trait and it was not until the 1960s that scholars began suggesting that *inequalities* and *disadvantages* in society were influential factors in youth offending and deviant behaviour. It was during this period of change (late 60s) that the Labour government, supported by social service agencies, began to attempt to transform the Youth Justice System from one that was based on *justice*, *control* and *punishment* to one based upon *welfare*, *care* and *treatment*. This philosophy was integrated into the *Children and Young Persons Act of 1969*, which was intended to create a radical new system for the treatment of young people. Unfortunately the planned phasing out of attendance centres and detention centres was abandoned by the Conservatives when they came to power in the 1970s and we see an increase in the imprisonment of young people.

Reflection point

The tensions between welfare and justice stem from a dichotomy that we have as a society. On the one hand young people have been portrayed as reckless gangs and they are demonised and treated accordingly, and on the other hand we have seen them as children in trouble, which has resulted in introducing practices embedded with sentiment. Think about your values and where you stand in this debate.

The *Criminal Justice Act 1991* had an impact on the Criminal Justice System as a whole and youth justice was not excluded from this radical overhaul. Again there was a shift in policy and legislation from *welfare*, *care* and *treatment* to a system of *justice*, *control* and *punishment*. One of the largest changes to the Youth Justice System was the Crime and Disorder Act 1998. This Act introduced the Youth Justice Board (at a national level) and placed a duty on local authorities to establish and fund multi-agency Youth Offending Teams (at a local level). Prior to this Act young people over the age of 16 (13 in some cases) were managed by the Probation Service. The 1998 Act established 'the prevention of offending' as the principal aim of youth justice and made it a statutory requirement of all those working in the youth justice system to have regard to this aim. The *Youth and Criminal Evidence Act 1999* continued the reforming process, it extended the use of Restorative Justice, introduced Referral Orders for first time offenders who have pleaded guilty, and engaged the community to sit as panel members. The *Criminal Justice and Immigration Act 2008* introduced the *Youth Rehabilitation Order*, which replaced all *Youth Community Orders*. Intensive Supervision and Surveillance was introduced as requirements of a Youth Rehabilitation Order and as an alternative to custody. *The Legal Aid Sentencing and Punishment of Offenders Act 2012* has introduced significant changes that affect the Youth Justice System concerning youth sentences, remands of children (otherwise than on bail), out-of-court disposals, knife crime and rehabilitation of offenders.

*S*enior Practitioner, 'The introduction of the Crime and Disorder Act was a key development in my career as it put meaningful structure in a fragmented system.'

Action point

Think about your views of young people.
What expectations do you have about young people?
What assumptions do you have about them?

Overview of the Youth Justice Board

Youth Offending Teams are guided by the Youth Justice Board. This board is an executive non-departmental body sponsored by the Ministry of Justice and receives funding from the Home Office and the Department of Education. Created to oversee the Youth Justice System it has other roles and functions, which include advising the Home Secretary on the operation of the Youth Justice System; promoting and monitoring effective practice; setting performance indicators; and commissioning research. The Youth Justice Teams work towards achieving the aims and objectives of the Youth Justice Board. These are:

Objective

• to prevent offending by children and young persons.

Aims

1 to reduce the number of first time entrants;
2 to reduce re-offending;
3 to reduce the use of custody and custodial remands.

Key figures and facts (Youth Justice Board)

• there are 158 Youth Offending Teams;
• these are grouped into 10 regional Teams;
• they come under the umbrella of the Ministry of Justice;
• they are overseen by a management board, which is chaired by a local authority Senior Official;
• they are viewed as a successful multi-agency model in terms of delivering public services;
• funding sources include the Youth Justice Board, Local Authorities and Local Agencies;
• local partnerships are made up of partners from:
    – Police Service
    – National Probation Service
    – local authority children's services (Education and Social Services)

- health services
- the Crown Prosecution Service.

Functions of the Youth Offending Teams

- Provide a service to young people to prevent them entering the Criminal Justice System; support them at the Police station in the form of an appropriate adult; undertake comprehensive assessments and prepare reports and sentence plans; supervise orders made by the court and deliver restorative justice interventions.
- Work alongside other agencies to ensure young people keep to acceptable behaviour contracts and antisocial behaviour orders.
- Target youth crime intervention programmes such as Youth Intensive Supervision Programmes to help support and direct young people away from crime.
- Work with higher risk young people, deliver programmes such as the knife crime programme or gang related crime.
- Offer reparation work to enable the young person to make amends, repay the community and help young people to understand the impact of their behaviour.
- Provide Restorative Justice Panels to bring offenders and victims together.

Youth Offender Team Officer, a brief description of their job: 'Supervision of young people on statutory Court Orders (Youth Rehabilitation orders, Referral Orders), completion of initial and on-going assessments (full assessment alongside assessment of harm posed to others, harm posed to themselves and risk of re-offending), co-ordination and delivery of interventions, instigation of breach proceedings in light of any non-compliance, presentation of reports for Referral Order Panels and court appearances. On-going motivational work used to encourage compliance and change in behaviours.'

Each area will differ in the structure of its service due to the
size of the team and the local area demands, so we advise you
to familiarise yourself with the structure of the area you may be
considering applying to.

Structure of the Youth Offending Teams

To give you an idea of the different employment and career
opportunities on offer we have selected an example collection of
the teams you may work in. These teams may be staffed by a
Team Manager, Senior Practitioners, Youth Offending Team
Officers, seconded Probation Officer and Specialist Education and
Substance misuse Workers.

Interventions team: This team has responsibility for the delivery
   of interventions such as group work and accredited programmes. They also cover sports engagement, Referral
   Orders and Restorative Justice. They organise and provide
   staffing support for referral panels, and recruit and support
   volunteers such as panel members and mentors.

Reducing custody team: This team has responsibility for the
   higher risk offenders; provides supervision for those on bail,
   through-care and post release support and intervention; and
   Intensive Supervision Orders.

Divisional teams: This team manages all those young people
   subject to community orders (and some lower risk in custody) and they will complete programmes on a one-to-one
   basis when needed.

Preventions team: This team works with those at risk of offending behaviour, referrals come from other agencies and the
   young people are engaged through one-to-one sessions and

activities. The team provides advice, guidance and support in the form of family interventions and a triage system. It will target a specified number of children and young people who are at risk of entering the Youth Justice System.

*S*enior Practitioner, What one piece of advice would you have for students who want to get into this sector? 'To look at the different types of roles there are within the YOS and seek out appropriate volunteering opportunities whilst they are still studying to confirm whether they enjoy the work and also give them work-related skills for their CV. Most people within the YOS started their careers in other specialist areas such as the Police, substance misuse workers, education workers, social workers, youth workers, housing etc. My chosen career was housing, I entered the Youth Offending Service following their job advertisement for a lead in Accommodation.'

Becoming a Youth Offending Team Officer

By now you will begin to have an understanding that the Youth Offending Team provides a wide range of services to young people who are at risk of offending or who have committed offences and been made subject to a court order or are on licence. The diverse composition of the multi-agency working model means that specialists work together in different capacities and carry out different roles depending on their remit. They have the common goal of working with young people to prevent and reduce crime and have therefore developed their knowledge and skills base to engage young people who are troubled. You could begin your career as a Youth Offending Team Officer; this includes both *non graduate* and *graduate* workers. Those referred to as '*Qualified Practitioners*' have higher education degrees in the subject areas of social work or probation qualifications and work as *Case Managers* or may be known as *Senior Practitioners*. Remember different titles are ascribed by different teams and regions.

Job description and entry requirement

Youth Offending Team Officer (YOTO Unqualified)

Entry requirement

The basic entry requirement for a Youth Offending Team Officer post requires that:

- you are over the age of 18;
- you are eligible to work in the UK;

- there are no minimum entry requirements but you would need to possess good literacy, numeracy, administrative and organisational skills;
- before being offered a post you must have clearance from the Disclosure and Barring Service.

Most positions require you work a 37-hour week, however from our knowledge of the Youth Offending Teams these posts require a *degree of flexibility*, and you may be required to work outside normal office hours, which may include evenings, weekends and bank holidays. Most positions require previous knowledge and experience of work with young people and this can be achieved by doing voluntary work. You must remember that these positions are subject to enhanced criminal record disclosure by the Disclosure and Barring Service, remember having a criminal record does not automatically bar you from working within the Youth Justice Teams as it depends on the nature of the conviction and the circumstances of the offence. Your situation will be assessed on an individual basis.

The job advertisement will identify a list of generic duties and a list of specific duties that would be integral in your role. Generic duties would include a requirement that you cover other duties not specific to your role. Some areas stipulate a requirement that you have possession of, or willingness and ability to complete, the Youth Justice Board Certificate in Effective Practice or an equivalent qualification. A basic job advertisement stipulates the following skills as essential.

Essential skills to work in this field

There are a range of skills required to work within the YOT and these will be specifically identified by the person specification, which outlines the requirements for the specific role you would be undertaking and for the vacancy being offered. We have compiled a list of skills that are common in the application forms.

- *The ability to engage and get on with young people.* Working with young people who are at risk and troubled can prove to be very challenging and developing the skills to engage and interact is essential for effective work. Some people have good communication with young people and this stems from having a genuine interest in working with them. Being enthusiastic and innovative is engaging and young people will respond positively to this style of working. This can be strengthened by having an understanding of the issues that affect young people.

- *Patience, empathy and non-judgemental attitude.* Working with young people can be very challenging and you must have the personal qualities to be able to deal with some difficult and demanding situations. This skill (and quality) can be developed and strengthened by having an understanding of the issues that affect young people.
- The ability to *stay calm when under pressure* is a good quality to possess and a skill that can be developed and strengthened.
- *Assessment skills* are a necessity in working in this field. You will need these skills to assess risks of harm both from and to the young person. You will use these assessment skills to identify the interventions suitable and make proposals to the court. Many young people are vulnerable and your assessment skills are essential when assessing risks they may face or in assessing the risks they may pose.
- *Good communication skills.* Not only will you need good, clear communication skills to engage young people but you will be engaging with their families, parents and carers. You will also need effective communication skills when dealing with other agencies in the process of information sharing and joint working in reducing re-offending.
- *Problem-solving skills* will enable you to engage with the young person and their family or carer to identify the issues they face. Working together to identify problems will enable you to jointly identify solutions and goals to overcome these problems.
- *Clear written communication skills* are essential as you will be required to prepare a range of different style reports. There are reports for the court, for referral order panels and for the parole board.

- *Good organisation skills.* You will need to manage your time effectively and prioritise tasks. Your time management skills will be required to maintain your diary commitments.

Action point

Working with children and young people requires engaging and interactive communication styles – can you think how these would be different from those of dealing with adults?

What do you think are the key considerations in starting a new professional relationship with a young person? Practise introducing yourself to a young person you are meeting for the first time.

Youth Offending Team Officer, Three things that I like about my job:

(1) It's varied – no two days are the same;

(2) Working out the balance between public protection and the welfare of children;

(3) The people I work with.

The application process

The ten Regional areas have responsibility for the recruitment and selection of their staff. Vacancies are advertised by the local Youth Offending Teams on their website, in the national and local media and in job centres. You would be required to contact the relevant human resources department and request an application pack. This will contain all the relevant information. In most areas there are two stages to the application process. First you will be required to complete an *application form* and this can be paper based or in an electronic format, check this with the local authority.

In completing the application form you must remember that you are given guidance on the skills, knowledge, experience and abilities that are required to fulfil the post. These are the criteria that are used in the selection process; you must demonstrate how you meet each of these criteria. You must also include your awareness, understanding and commitment to equality and diversity in employment and service delivery. Failure to demonstrate these will reduce your chances of being short-listed.

If you are successfully short-listed you will proceeded to the next stage and you will be invited for interview. Remember you will need to demonstrate the essential skills we covered earlier on in the chapter.

Working as a Youth Offending Team Officer

Following successful interview, you would join the local authority Youth Offending Team. You will be allocated a specific role and carry out specified duties dependant on the post you take. You will be supported through the induction process and as your knowledge of the systems grows so will your caseload and responsibilities. We have listed a range of duties and roles you may carry out such as assessing risks and preparing reports. Let us look at a specific role.

In order to work effectively with young people you would have to agree an *Action Plan* that is aimed at reducing re-offending. This action plan would be drawn up in detail identifying a *series of interventions* to address offending behaviour, following a comprehensive assessment. *Assessment skills* are needed not only to assess risks but also to build up a picture of the young person you are working with. You, as the young person's Officer, would *supervise these interventions*. Now this plan could include practical actions like a *referral to specialist agencies* such as substance misuse services or accommodation providers. It would include *offence focussed work* and require you to carry out *one-to-one programmes* to help the young person understand why they offend. This would also help them to *develop strategies and skills* to avoid getting into difficult situations that result in offending in the future. You may be required to *engage with the parents or carers* of the young person in order to understand the current situation and also to help support change. Remember you may *also visit young people in secure institutions* and be involved in the *risk assessment process and planning* after their release.

---

*Y*outh Offending Team Officer, 'Three things that I like about my job:

(1) Motivational work undertaken to encourage compliance;

(2) Moving young people onto post-16 training and employment opportunities;

(3) Opportunity to still deliver one-to-one offending behaviour interventions.'

Career development opportunities

While working as a Youth Offending Team Officer you will be encouraged to work towards recognised qualifications. This will provide an excellent opportunity to develop your professional skills and knowledge base in the area of Youth Justice. Professional skills development is supported by the Youth Justice Board and, in corroboration with the Open University, they have developed the *Youth Justice Interactive Learning Space*. This is an e-learning environment where staff can access a range of learning resources, assessment tools, course material and exchange information. This facility is available to all staff who are employed by or are a volunteer of the Service.

Action point

If you are currently working as volunteer or in the Youth Justice Service you will have access to the Youth Justice Interactive learning Space at www.yjils.org.uk.

As a *non graduate* you may wish to develop your career opportunities further and improve your knowledge and skills base by completing a *Certificate in Youth Justice*. This course will provide you with the basic knowledge and skills required of a Youth Justice worker and as it is a vocationally orientated programme it could be the starting point to your career path of attending university and completing a relevant degree.

Action point

The Certificate of Higher Education in Youth Justice is a vocationally orientated academic award. Take a look at the Open University website for more information at www.open.ac.uk.

There is also the *Youth Justice Effective Practice Certificate*, which is an approved learning programme available to those working within the Youth Justice System. This certificate was commissioned by the Youth Justice Board and endorsed by the Skills for Justice Awards. The programme is designed to enable practitioners to consider how to make informed decisions when working with young people in the Youth Justice System. The programme is structured to link research, theory and practice in youth justice and is delivered in six modules.

For those of you who have entered the Youth Justice Team as a *graduate*, after gaining valuable experience as a Youth Offending Team Worker you may wish to consider completing a post-graduate qualification in social work. To apply for the social work course, you must have relevant practical experience and this would put you in a strong position.

Qualified Senior Practitioners/Case Managers

It is important to recognise that the wide range of skills and knowledge you have accumulated while working as a Youth Offending Team Officer, a volunteer or on your university programme, is highly transferable. All operational teams have a Senior Practitioner in the team. Some current Senior Practitioners have social work or relevant degrees and qualifications in their area of expertise. But remember when applying for the post of Senior Practitioner you will have some staff management responsibilities as an integral part of the role.

The recruitment process

It is becoming increasingly essential to have a Social Work or Probation Officer Qualification to apply for the position of Senior Practitioner. The posts will be advertised in both the local and national newspapers and local authority youth justice websites. It is important to familiarise yourself with the local requirements and details of the available vacancy. This post requires you to work a 37-hour week but as you should already be aware, there is a degree of flexibility needed and you may have to be available to work out of hours and weekends. Working as a qualified Senior Practitioner has a starting salary of £34,000–£40,000.

Knowledge and skills

Senior Practitioner, 'What are the three most important skills you use at work?

(1) communication
(2) problem solving
(3) decision-making.'

The list below has been composed from recent job advertisements that list the essential skills and knowledge for the post.

working in youth justice

You would need to demonstrate that you meet these requirements in both your application form and during competitive interview:

- CQSW or DipSW or equivalent relevant professional/graduate level qualification;
- General Social Care Council Registration as a Registered social worker;
- evidence of associated post qualifying training;
- a minimum of two years' post qualifying and front line professional experience with exposure to a wide ranging field of practice. At least one year must have been spent within a child/young person centred service, thus ensuring a sound understanding of the services available to children and young people who commit criminal offences;
- significant experience working with children and young people who offend and an understanding of the issues that affect young people and children;
- detailed understanding of national children's policy;
- knowledge and understanding of child protection procedures and ECC policies;
- knowledge and understating of child development theories and family dynamics and systems;
- information technology competent with evidence of high quality case recording;
- self-awareness of own strengths and areas for development and a commitment to continuous professional development;
- ability to challenge young people, their attitudes and behaviours in an appropriate and positive manner;
- a commitment to working in partnership with young people, their parents/carers and others involved in the young person's life;
- a commitment to anti-oppressive practice, behaviour and management.

Senior Practitioner (brief description of what you do): 'Manage 2 x full time staff; manage a pool of approximately 15 sessional workers; manage a pool of 30 volunteer mentors; support and staff several sports engagement sessions; quality assure Referral Order reports; staff Referral Order Panels; co-ordinate the service's AQA (Assurance and Quality Alliance) certificate programme; manage budgets; lead by example!!'

Becoming a Youth Offending Team Manager

The Youth Offending Service offers you an excellent opportunity for career progression. You will need to be in post for about three to five years post-qualifying as you will need to have the experience to develop the skills and knowledge to manage a team and be directly responsible for managerial, financial and policy issues. Remember that this is a profession where promotion takes you away from hands-on work with young people as you will be managing other social workers. Most team managers have social work qualifications as there are safeguarding issues and decisions to make that need the theoretical and policy-knowledge base of a qualified practitioner.

*T*eam Manager, '(What I wish I had known when I was choosing my career) is that you can move up to management quickly but you lose the contact with clients, which is what attracted you in the first place. This takes some adjustment.'

Action point

Think about a time when you had to take responsibility (like lead a team):

- What did you do?
- What happened?

- What was your role?
- What did it feel like?
- What did you learn about yourself from the experience?

The Youth Justice System in Northern Ireland

Brief overview

The Youth Justice System in Northern Ireland offers similar opportunities for working with young people who have committed offences as those in the rest of the UK. There are some differences; the main one is that of the *central* role Restorative Justice plays in the response to youth crime in Northern Ireland. Restorative Justice offers an *inclusive problem-solving response* to young people who offend and gives them the opportunity to put right the harms caused to the victim. For this reason we have chosen to consider the role of the Youth Justice Conference Co-ordinator. It is important when applying for a post with an organisation to have an awareness of its origins and historical developments and this will also put the employment options into some perspective.

Historically the Youth Justice System in Northern Ireland was shaped by the legislative and policy developments in England and Wales. In 1998, following the Criminal Justice Review Group, legislation diverged and was developed in a different direction from that in the England and Wales model (The Criminal Justice Review was set up following the Good Friday Agreement 1998). The 2000 Review recommended widespread introduction of *community based Restorative Justice Practices* for young people between the ages of ten and seventeen. These recommendations were put into legislation under the *Justice (Northern Ireland) Act 2002*. The changes included setting out the *aims of youth justice*, the inclusion of *new community and custodial orders* and the establishment of the whole new system of youth conferences based around the principles of *Restorative Justice*. In 2003 the *National Youth Justice Agency* was established as an executive agency to replace the former *Juvenile*

Justice Board and to administer the Youth Justice Services and oversee the range of new disposals available to the courts; these include Reparation Orders, Community Disposal Orders and Youth Conference Orders.

Action point

Review what you read in Chapter 2 of this text as a reminder of the similarities and differences in the Northern Irish Criminal Justice System to England and Wales.

Reflection point

Earlier Youth Justice Services were shaped by the troubles in Northern Ireland. Due to a culture of suspicion towards authority many interventions have been developed and delivered in the community by the voluntary sector services rather than the core State provision. This continues and the Youth Justice System is supported by an active voluntary and community sector. Consider approaching these organisations for both voluntary work and paid employment.

The National Youth Justice Agency (NI)

When considering a career as a Youth Justice Service practitioner you would be employed by the National Youth Justice Agency. There are a number of professional roles for graduates and non graduates working in the teams similar to the UK systems. When looking towards a career in this field you need to be fully aware of the Agency's aims and values, as these will inform your practice and will be integral to the recruitment and selection process.

Mission statement

Making communities safer by helping children to stop offending.

Values

- We will deliver services to young people based on proportionality and individually assessed risks, needs and ability.
- We will work to change, challenge and support young people to be the best they can be.
- We will hold young people to account for their offending and, where possible, young people should make good the harm they have done.
- We will use research and evidence based practice to inform all our work.
- We respect everyone no matter how different they are.
- Everything we do will be underpinned by equality, openness, fairness, honesty and integrity.
- The Agency provides a range of services both within the community and within custody and often delivers these services in partnership with others, with the aims of:
  - helping children to address their offending behaviour;
  - diverting them from crime;
  - assisting their integration into the community; and
  - meeting the needs of the victims of crime.

Key facts (Youth Justice Agency Northern Ireland)

- the Agency employs around 350 staff;
- the Agency has an annual budget of approximately £20 million;
- there are eight local area offices across with responsibility for:
  - supervising young people subject to a range of court orders;
  - delivering youth conferences;
  - delivering programmes and interventions with young people and their parents/carers to prevent re-offending.

The role of a Youth Justice Service Practitioner has *similar positions* to those roles discussed in the earlier part of this text. One role that is distinctly different is that of the Youth Conference Co-ordinator. We will consider this as the career option in this section.

The Youth Justice Directorate of the Youth Justice Agency

As part of the wider Youth Justice Agency, the Youth Justice Directorate has the role of managing the implementation of youth conferencing in Northern Ireland. These conferences provide the opportunity for the young person and the victim to meet and make amends in the form of an apology and some form of reparation. There are two types of conference; a diversionary and a court ordered conference, both require the youth Conference Co-ordinator to provide a recommendation to the Court or Prosecutor of how to proceed.

Action point

Taking a look at the website, it will give you more in-depth information about the functions and the roles of the Conferences – www.youthjusticeagencyni.gov.uk.

There are opportunities to achieve post-graduate qualifications in Restorative Justice. You can do this on a part time basis and the requirements are: currently in relevant employment and you have a relevant degree (or equivalent qualification). See the University of Ulster's website for more information at www.ulster.ac.uk.

The role of the Youth Conference Coordinator

- make preparation for the conference to take place;
- facilitate the conference processes, to ensure the young person and victims are fully aware of the process and stages;
- act as a support for the young person in completing the final conference plan;
- draw up an action plan for the young person;
- supervise the plan;
- refer the plan back to court in the event of non-co-operation.

You must hold a professional qualification to undertake the role of Youth Conference Co-ordinator. The majority of those currently employed have progressed through the Youth Practitioner role and some have probation backgrounds. Vacancies for this post only occasionally become available as those in post love the job. When they do arise they will be advertised on the Youth Justice Agency website.

The Youth Justice System in Scotland

For those of you considering a career in the Youth Justice Services in Scotland it is important to understand that there are similarities with and differences from the systems in England, Wales and Northern Ireland. The Youth Justice Services in Scotland is a range of practices and procedures for dealing with young people who may be at risk of becoming involved, or are engaged in, offending behaviour. A major *difference* is all children in Scotland are dealt with by one single agency and those young people who are subject to compulsory measures because of offending behaviour are considered *Children in Need* or *Looked after Children*. Since the 1960s the provisions for services in Scotland have been developed based on the notion that they are first and foremost children. The Children's Hearing System is at the core of the Youth Justice Service, it deals with children between the ages of eight and twelve (who cannot be prosecuted in the criminal courts) and children aged twelve and over (who can be prosecuted in the criminal courts) on both offence and non-offence grounds. Young people who appear at the hearing system are dealt with by the local Children and Families Service and those with more complex or serious offending patterns may be dealt with by the local council Youth Justice Team. Please note there may be slight variations depending on the local authority delivery guidance. The *similarities* with the Services in the UK are that Youth Justice Services are delivered by both unqualified and qualified social work staff in a style of multi-agency and multi-disciplinary Operational Teams.

Reflection point

It is not the aim of this chapter to consider the different systems but to provide an outline of the career opportunities in the field of Youth Justice in Scotland.

Some areas call them Youth Justice Teams, in some they are known as Youth Action Teams.

Overview of the Scottish Youth Justice System

It is important to understand the historical developments of the agency you may be considering as a prospective career path. The Youth Justice System in Scotland had its most radical overhaul in the 1960s when services for young people moved from a court system to a tribunal system based on the welfare of the child. The Kilbrandon Review (1964) acknowledged that offending by young people was a consequence of complex individual and family issues and the interest of the child was paramount in any intervention. With this in mind one single agency was established to deal with *all children*. By 1968 the Juvenile Courts were abolished, and the *Children's Hearing System* was introduced in 1971. This informal tribunal consists of three Panel Members from the local community and a Children's Reporter. Children and Young People up to the age of 17 (16–17 is rare) can be referred from a number of concerned agencies. The *1995 Children's Act* saw a shift in the welfare model and introduced the notion of risk posed by children. Since then, a range of policies, action plans and legislation has introduced the notion of responsibility and accountability in the form of new orders for young people who offend.

Action point

There are a range of systems that you should make yourself aware of. Take a look at the relevant websites for more detailed explanations:

The Children's Hearing System www.chscotland.gov.uk

The Kilbrandon Review and the Getting It Right For Every Child (GIRFEC) are explained on the Scottish government website site. Access this at www.Scotland.gov.uk and familiarise yourself with the relevant documentation.

Deciding on a career path in Youth Justice in Scotland will give you the opportunity to enter through a range of entry routes and you could begin your career as a non graduate or a graduate. This would offer you similar career opportunities and skills development as those discussed earlier in the chapter. For those wishing to qualify as a Criminal Justice Youth Worker (social worker) you would need to achieve the social work qualification.

Key roles

The multi-disciplinary Youth Justice Team/Youth Action Teams include a combination of the same agencies as those in the rest of the UK.

Objectives

The Youth Justice Provision in Scotland aims to:

• provide quality youth justice processes and practice;

- provide an appropriate range and availability of interventions for children and young people involved in offending behaviour;
- promote early and effective intervention;
- ease the transition between the Children's Hearing and adult Criminal Justice Systems;
- ensure that secure accommodation and detention is used only when it is the most appropriate disposal and that consideration has been given to alternatives;
- improve information and assistance provided to victims of youth offending and local communities;
- provide strategic direction and co-ordination of multi-disciplinary services for children and young people who offend through locality planning and performance improvements.

Should you wish to enter the Criminal Justice Youth Offending Team you would benefit from revisiting the Scottish Probation Section on becoming a Criminal Justice social worker and linking the skills and entry requirements from earlier sections in this chapter. We will consider the alternative career structure available to working in the Scottish Youth services, and this is working within the *Scottish Children's Reporter Administration*. There are a range of roles you may wish to consider from Support Assistant, Support Administrator, Locality Support Manager and Reporter. This section will consider the role of the Children's Reporter.

Working in the Scottish Children's Reporter Administration (SCRA)

The Children's Hearing System is the Care and Justice System for Scotland's children and young people. A fundamental principle is that children who commit offences, and children who need care and protection, are dealt with in the same system – as they are often the same children (SCRA 2014). An integral part of the hearing system is the *Children's Reporter*. Employed by the Scottish Children's Reporter Administration, they receive referrals from a range of sources including teachers, Police and social workers.

The role and purpose of the Scottish Children's
Reporter Administration is to

- make effective decisions about a need to refer a child to a Children's Hearing;
- enable children and families to participate in the Children's Hearing;
- provide suitable accommodation and facilities for Children's Hearings;
- disseminate information and data to inform and influence improved outcomes for children and young people.

Action point

Revisit the Children's Hearing System at www.chscotland.
gov.uk and familiarise yourself with the service it provides
to the Scottish government. Read the vision statement and
note the values and service standards that aim to achieve
this vision. There is a section for newly qualified social
workers that helps practitioners explain the system to young
people – this may be useful.

Now write your vision for young people and then list your
values.

How well does your statement and list match up with that
of the Scottish Children's Reporter Administration?

Key facts in 2012/13 (Scottish Children's Reporter
Administration)

- the SCRA has nine localities;
- 22,561 children referred to the Reporter;
- 2.5 per cent of all children in Scotland;
- two categories of referral:
  - care and protection grounds
  - offence;
- most common referral is 'lack of parental care' and victim of Schedule 1 offence;
- 38,316 Children's Hearings held.

Becoming a Reporter

To become a Children's Reporter you must hold a relevant qualification such as a social work or a Law degree and it is essential that you have experience of working with children. As a Reporter you would have responsibility for receiving and investigating the cases referred to you. You may request further detailed reports, from social workers or teachers, to help in your assessment. You would then reach a decision on whether the young person would benefit from attending a Hearing. For some young people a Hearing may not be required (i.e. supportive families) but for those assessed as being in need of help and support you would request they attend a Hearing. It is your duty to attend all Hearings and record the outcomes reached by the Panel. There are occasions where you would be required to prepare and present cases to court.

Reflection point

Hearings are run by Panel Members who are specially selected and trained volunteers from the local community. They give up their time, talk to the young people and their families and reach a decision to help the young person improve their situation. Do a search of the web; there are some interesting media articles and reports on the Panel.

How to apply to become a Reporter

The Scottish Children's Reporter Administration advertise their vacancies on their recruitment website and in the local and regional media, so it is advisable to familiarise yourself with the local job advertisement – check regularly. The role requires you to work 35 hours a week but there is a need to be flexible as some Hearings may be held of an evening. You can expect to begin on a starting salary of between £32,000 and £39,000. The following are essential requirements:

Eligibility

You must be eligible to work in Scotland.

Qualifications

- a degree in Social Work, Law, Education or other relevant discipline;
- you must have evidence of continuing professional development.

Experience

- you must have a minimum of two years' work experience in a related field;
- and knowledge and experience of partnership working.

Essential skills and knowledge

- understanding of the Children's Hearing System, the roles and responsibilities of other involved agencies and issues affecting it;
- understanding of children's needs;
- assessment, investigative and interviewing skills;
- effective communication skills;
- ability to work effectively as part of a team;
- ability to plan and prioritise work;
- ability to work to deadlines and statutory requirements;
- ability to handle sensitive situations with tact and diplomacy;
- ability to exercise judgement and make decisions.

Action point

If you know you possess the qualifications, have the experience and the skills and knowledge to fulfil this role, and you are motivated to develop your career along this path you would be advised to contact the SCRA and have an

working in youth justice

informal discussion. Take a look at the SCRA website (www.scra.gov.uk), familiarise yourself with the role further and contact the relevant named person for an informal discussion.

Chapter summary

Having read the chapter you will hopefully have a clearer understanding of the Youth Justice Service and the Youth Offending Teams in the UK. You will have some knowledge of the structure and the roles and you will have gained insight into the application process. Completing some of the action and reflection points will give you more information and help you know if this is the field that you would like to work in and develop a career with.

Top tips

- Think of your contribution to a team.
- How do you know you have communicated effectively?
- How do you make your degree relevant?
- What is the core focus of your dissertation/work-based learning project?
- How can you evidence your skills?
- Understand the organisation.
- Take time to read and familiarise yourself with the recruitment process.
- Give yourself time to complete the application form correctly.
- Practise your communication skills.
- Understand the assessment criteria.
- Know the difference between essential and desirable selection criteria.

working in youth justice   269

- Practise your presentation skills; including your non-verbal communication.
- Be aware of your values and motivations.
- Think about why you want the job that you have applied for.

Some useful websites

These websites will give you some useful information for volunteering opportunities in the different areas:

England – www.volunteering.org.uk
Scotland – www.volunteerscotland.net
NI – www.volunteernow.co.uk
Wales – www.volunteering-wales.net

These websites will give you further detailed information on the declaration of criminal convictions:

- www.gov.uk (Disclosure and barring service in England and Wales)
- www.disclosurescotland.co.uk (for Scotland)
- www.dojni.gov.uk (for the Access (NI) Northern Ireland Site)

Recommended reading

Campbell, C., Devlin, R., O'Mahony, D., Doak, J., Jackson, J., Corrigan, T. and McEvoy, K. (2005) *Evaluation of the Northern Ireland Youth Conference Service*. NIO Research and Statistical Series: Report No. 12. Institute of Criminology and Criminal Justice, School of Law, Queen's University, Belfast

Haydon, D. (2009) Developing a Manifesto for Youth Justice in Northern Ireland: Background Paper. Belfast: Include Youth

McVie, S. (n.d) Alternative Models of Youth Justice: Lessons from Scotland and Northern Ireland. Retrieved from the University of Edinburgh website www.research.ed.ac.uk/portal/files/8644714/alternative_models_of_youth_justice.pdf (accessed 27 May 2014)

Maruna, S. (n.d.) Youth Justice Review. Annotated Bibliography of Northern Ireland-Based Research on Youth Justice Issues. Retrieved

working in youth justice

from Queen's University Belfast www.dojni.gov.uk/index/
publications/publication-categories/pubs-criminal-justice/youth-
justice-review/s-maruna-annotated-bibliography-of-ni-based-research-
on-youth-justice-issues.pdf (accessed 27 May 2014)

Muncie, J. (2009) *Youth and Crime*. London: Sage

Perrott, S. (16 Jan 2012) Youth Justice: A look at how Northern
Ireland's approach to young offenders. Retrieved from www.
holyrood.com/2012/01/youth-justice-a-look-at-how-northern-
irelands-approach-to-young-offenders (accessed 27 May 2014)

References

SCRA Scottish Children's Reporter Administration (2014) *The
Children's Hearing System*. Retrieved from www.scra.gov.uk/sites/
scra/cms_resources/Social%20Work%20Protocol%20ebook.html
(accessed 27 May 2014)

Youth Justice Board for England and Wales (n.d) *About the Youth Justice
Board*. Retrieved from www.justice.gov.uk (accessed 27 May 2014)

Youth Justice Agency Northern Ireland (n.d) About Us. Retrieved from
www.youthjusticeagencyni.gov.uk/about_us (accessed 27 May 2014)

chapter 10

Alternative options

Pursuing other careers in Criminal Justice

Chapter objectives

By the end of this chapter you should be able to:

- identify a range of other career opportunities related to the Criminal Justice sector;
- identify the resources available for each of the sectors discussed.

This chapter will consider some alternative career paths that you may not have thought about that are all related to an interest in the field of Criminal Justice. We have chosen the areas of substance misuse, victim support, Social Services, Security Services, academia and forensic psychology because these are the 'alternative' careers that students currently studying Criminal Justice have expressed an interest in. It is intended that this chapter will provide a more general discussion of the jobs, roles and recruitment processes that apply and will not be restricted to a discussion on England and Wales, Scotland or Northern Ireland.

At this point we would like to acknowledge that the third sector, including the voluntary sector and the not for profit sector, has an increasing role to play in the work of the Criminal Justice System and offers a large and broad range of employment opportunities. The work of these organisations exists to help the statutory services meet their aims and objectives and support the work with both offenders and victims. Due to the wide variety of work and organisations in this sector we have decided not to focus specifically on it but would recommend that you look at the useful websites at the end of the text for further information and think as you read this chapter how the work of those working with drug users or in victim services may fit into this area.

Working in the substance misuse services

Working with individuals who misuse substances is a very challenging but rewarding career. The term substance misuse is used to describe the excessive use and misuse of substances such as drugs and alcohol. There are a range of different organisations you could begin or continue a career in. These fall into two sectors, government-funded organisations that work in partnership with Criminal Justice organisations and voluntary organisations known as grass roots services. Government-funded organisations have a statutory requirement to work across services such as probation, health care, drug treatment and rehabilitation services. These statutory arrangements are part of the government's key strategy to combat drug and alcohol related crime. The funding of voluntary organisations is time limited and they rely heavily on voluntary work to maintain a support service for those with chronic substance misuse.

Reflection point

Think of the terms used to describe those who misuse substances. How much do you know about alcohol and drugs? How much do you know about the term addiction?

Working as a substance misuse worker would see you working in a range of drug and alcohol services helping individuals recover from addiction.

Roles

- working in close liaison with the Criminal Justice Agencies;
- work as part of a multi-agency provision in relation to prolific and priority offenders and integrated offender management model;
- working in the custody suit providing advice and support to those detailed or taking samples;
- working in rehabilitation and recovery; providing practical support and advice within a clinical setting. Completing one-to-one or group work interventions; providing help and support;
- supporting service users with their education and training;
- being an advocate;
- providing drop in services, supporting individuals who come to your agency either on a first time basis or on a regular 'ad hoc' basis;
- working in detoxification services; providing advice, counselling and structured programmes of intervention;
- working in outreach services; working with those individuals who often fall through the net of social care such as rough sleepers, sex workers and street drinkers.

Qualifications

It would depend on the agency and role you are considering applying for. Employers from the voluntary, private and statutory agencies would require you to have some working knowledge in this field. You would get this experience from doing voluntary work in the related sector. There are posts that require relevant professional qualifications for roles of responsibility. These qualifications could include social work, Criminal Justice or in the health care profession.

Skills and qualities required

You have to be motivated to work with individuals who are substance dependant. You must:

- be able to show empathy, warmth and caring.
- be non judgemental;
- have good problem-solving skills;
- have good assessment and care planning skills;
- have good communication skills to work with service uses and multi professionals;
- be prepared to work in drug and alcohol testing;
- have an understanding of the effects of substances on the personal, health and social impact on an individual.

Requirements

Although you may be contracted to work between 37 and 40 hours, many of these posts require a flexible approach to working and you will need to familiarise yourself with the requirements of the agency or organisation you are considering joining. It is difficult to pin point a specific salary, some starting salaries are £14,000 upwards, while others may begin at £20,000. The salary is dependent on the agency, position and role.

Reflection point

Working in the Drug Intervention Programme means you will be an integral part of the Integrated Offender Management Teams, which consist of the Police, probation, youth justice, mental health workers, electronic monitoring and employment services third sector providers. However, working in a voluntary organisation may see you working with those individuals who are in crisis and not stable enough to access the more prominent and statutory agencies. Take a look at some of the voluntary organisations in your area.

Working in Victim Support Services

The Victim Services provide an essential function within the Criminal Justice System and excellent career opportunities for those who have the skills and qualities to deliver practical advice and emotional support to victims of crime. There has been a significant shift in the focus of the Criminal Justice System, from a system focussed on the offender to one that has placed the victim centre-stage. Victims and witnesses are an essential component in the administration of justice, without whom the Criminal Justice System would not function. Becoming a victim can be an emotional and traumatic experience and victim support is one of the largest agencies that provide the essential support services they need.

Victim support is the largest victim's organisation of its kind; it is an independent charity that provides the practical and emotional support for victims and witnesses. Trained volunteers deliver its core services.

Working as a Victim Support Officer

You may need a minimum of one or two years' volunteering before you would be considered suitable for this role. The main duties include:

- receive referrals;
- contact victims;
- assess needs and develop plans of action;
- undertake direct victim work as required;
- provide support for people who have experienced crime;
- provide support for those who may have witnessed a crime and may be required to attend court;
- establish and maintain working relationships;
- complete home visits;
- maintain confidentiality;
- have an awareness of safeguarding policies and procedures;
- keep accurate and relevant up-to-date records;
- be responsible for your work case load;
- work in partnership.

Remember as a Victim Support Officer you will be provided with on-the-job training to develop and enhance both the essential skills and to develop areas of specialism such as working with survivors of domestic abuse and sexual violence.

Qualifications

There are a range of roles in the Victim Support Agency, some positions do not require qualifications but do prefer applicants to have experience in this field. You can gain valuable experience through volunteering in a range of capacities. You can volunteer with one of the victim support organisations, gain experience volunteering or working with vulnerable individuals in a counselling role or the Criminal Justice System.

Reflection point

To become a *volunteer* you must be 18 or over but you must also be mindful that working in these roles requires a level of maturity, resilience and integrity.

Revisit Chapter 4 and read the relevant section on volunteering. You may need a minimum of one or two years' volunteering before you would be considered for a Victim Support Officer.

Skills

You will need to demonstrate that you:

- have good listening skills and you are able to deal with people in a sensitive way;
- have the ability to provide support and guidance;
- have good communication skills both face-to-face and telephone skills;
- have a good understanding of confidentiality and safe-guarding issues and policies;

- have an ability to interact with people from a range of backgrounds and professions;
- can remain calm and rational in a range of crises and complex situations;
- have a non-judgemental and empathetic manner;
- have good problem-solving skills;
- have good reporting, recording skills and IT skills.

Requirements and salary

You would be required to work 37 hours a week and you must be prepared to work unsociable hours as you may be required to work outside the 9–5 to meet the demands of the role. In researching the employment opportunities for this chapter, the majority of roles were offered on a part-time flexible-hours basis, therefore pay is pro rata. The Victim Support Services note that the starting salaries are £15,000–£20,000, rising with experience.

Reflection point

There are a range of victim agencies providing support to victims of specific offences such as The Women's Aid. Research the different organisations and your skills in matching the suitability for both voluntary posts and vacancies.

Working in Social Services

Choosing a career in the Social Services sector is a rewarding, responsible and demanding position. Becoming involved in someone else's life to empower and support them to improve their life can be very challenging. It also provides opportunities for developing skills, obtaining qualifications and offering a career. This section will identify some roles within the Social Services sector and highlight some areas for further information before focussing on social work roles.

Working in Social Service roles

There are many different jobs within the Social Services that span the local authorities and the private and voluntary sectors. Different positions require different skill-sets; these skills will be developed while working with children and families, youth services, older people, a community development worker and mental health services. Some examples of roles include:

- *Youth and community worker* – working with young people to help them develop the skills to become more confident and reach their full potential.
- *Education welfare officer* – working with schools, families and young people to identify the issues that may be creating barriers to attendance and achievement, and working to seek solutions through relationship building, practical advice and support.
- *Early education/childcare* – there are many children and young people whose behaviour may be of concern. Following investigations it may be as a result of family issues and that the family need support in functioning as a family unit.

Action point

If you are seriously considering a career in the field of *Social Care* take a look at the skills for care website www.skills forcare.org.uk, this will provide some clear guidance as to the different roles, skills and career paths. Take the online quiz to see if this position suits you; access the resource at www.aquestionofcare.org.uk, this will help you think about your responses to a range of different situations.

Reflection point

Skills for Care are the responsible body for the training standards and development needs of social work and social care staff working in a range of sectors in England. Take a look at the website and familiarise yourself with these standards. You can access other responsible authorities at the following websites;

Scottish Social Care Council www.sssc.uk.com
Care Council for Wales www.ccwales.org.uk
Northern Ireland Social Care Council website www.niscc.info

Working as a social worker

To gain entry into social work there are a number of routes; you could begin your career as both a *non-graduate* or a *graduate*. It is important to recognise that this work involves working with many people who are facing a crisis; this could require long-term or short-term packages of care. Social workers can be employed across the range of private, voluntary and public services and are guided by legislation, policy and good practice procedures.

Reflection point

Take a look back through Chapter 5 (probation) and Chapter 9 (youth justice) for a more in-depth look at the roles a social worker could fulfil.

Unqualified

Social work assistant – This post would be suitable for both non-graduates and graduates wishing to begin their careers in this field. Depending on the field you entered, your role would be varied and include supporting people in the community and working alongside qualified practitioners. As a guideline you would work 37 hours a week and a starting salary could be between £12,500 and £17,000 a year. Taking advantage of the training and qualifications on offer, your salary could rise to between £17,000 and £22,000.

Entry requirements

Although not essential, it is desirable to have some experience of working in the caring services, this could be either voluntary or paid. You will be offered in-service training opportunities and should you wish to follow this career progression you would benefit from completing the relevant qualifications on offer and for non-graduates you may consider completing a degree.

Action point

Skills for care have a tool that will help you link your skills and identify options for your career pathway. Complete the Career Matrix to give you some ideas.

Action point

To become a social worker you must achieve the relevant qualifications. Take a look at the courses on offer in your region.

Qualified

The area of social work is vast and while on the programme of study you will have the opportunity to consider the range of posts, undertake practice placements and consider the area you wish to enter. You must also be realistic and acknowledge that some areas of social work generate higher turnover of staff and thus offer regular opportunities to work in services such as front-line *Child Protection* work. As a guide you could expect to earn a starting salary between £19,500 and £25,000 a year. As your experience, knowledge and responsibility increases you could expect to earn up to £40,000. Although most posts would offer regular working hours, it is our experience that you must be flexible as managing complex situations does not just happen during office hours.

Working in the Security Services

If you are interested in developing a career in the security sector there are a range of roles and career options you may wish to consider. This section will briefly consider the different career opportunities available in the government agency, *the Security Services*, better known as MI5, and the opportunities offered by the *private security sector*.

The Security Service MI5

The Security Services has had a range of names but is more commonly known by its short alternative MI5. It is the UK's national security intelligence agency and works to 'counter terrorism, foreign espionage and weapons proliferation'. The main role of MI5 is to gather information about organisations that may pose a threat to the UK's national security. This secret intelligence is gathered through covert operations and the information is then assessed and investigated in close corroboration with other government departments and foreign security and intelligence services.

Some key facts and figures (MI5 website)

The Guardian UK 300 2012/2013 survey reported that MI5 is the:

- ninth most popular graduate employer overall;
- third most popular employer in the public sector;
- eighth most popular among those wanting to work in IT and technology;
- tenth most popular with female final year university students.

MI5 staffing figures (2012/13)

- 3,9000 employees;
- 40 per cent of staff are women;
- 55 per cent of staff are less than 40 years old;
- 8 per cent of staff are from black or ethnic minority backgrounds;

- 3 per cent of staff have reported a disability;
- 350 are secondment or attachment from other departments.

Roles

MI5 employ a wide range of people from a variety of backgrounds to work in many different positions. There are a range of roles you could apply from including Administration Assistants; Business Support Officers; Foreign Language Analysts; to Intelligence Officers. All of these roles have specific skills and knowledge requirements. For example as a *Mobile Surveillance Officer*, you would be required to follow someone on foot or in a car, you need to be quick thinking, fit comfortably into many different environments and use your observation skills to note details.

Action point

You would benefit from taking a look at the MI5 website. Give yourself plenty of time to read about the organisation, its functions, aims and values. Then take a close look at the different roles and as you work your way through them take the various challenges and test your skills. These challenges are designed to help you understand if you would be suited to the different posts.

MI5 offer a specific *graduate* route on the Intelligence Officer Development Programme. Not only are they looking for highly capable and confident graduates but you must have analytical skills, good communication skills and be a team player.

Eligibility

You must be a British citizen to work for the Security Service. One of your parents should also be British or have substantial ties to the UK. You must be resident in the UK nine out of the last ten years.

Salaries

As a graduate recruited to MI5 you would expect to begin on a salary ranging from £25,056 for Intelligence Officers and Intelligence (Data) Analysts and £27,613 for Digital Intelligence Officers.

Application process

The recruitment process lasts at least six months due to the lengthy vetting process that takes place. You can only apply for one post at a time and you can not apply for the same role more than once in a twelve month period. Familiarise yourself with the different roles and the application process by spending time on their website.

Reflection point

What are the differences between the Security Services (MI5) and the Secret Intelligent Services (MI6)? Look at the MI6 website, take their intelligence test. Do you have the skills to consider a career with MI6?

Private security companies

The Private Security Sector offers a wide range of employment and career opportunities. It is a sector that continues to experience rapid growth in the UK, due to the increase in both the public and private companies investing large amounts of money in the protection and security of their staff, property and data. This sector also works closely with the Police Services and may provide those functions that do not require Police powers.

The Security Industry Association (SIA) is the main organisation that has responsibility for overseeing the UK's security industry. It has the responsibility for licensing individuals who work in specific roles. In order to obtain a licence, you must provide proof of your identity, address and relevant qualifications (if required). They will also complete the required criminal records check to confirm suitability to hold the relevant licence. The licence currently costs around £220. Roles that need a licence to work include: CCTV Operator, Security Guard, Cash and Valuables in Transit, Door Supervisor and Mobile Patrol Officer.

Reflection point

Look at the *Security Industry Authority* website for details about employment options and in-depth licensing requirements. *The Security Institute* details the different professional qualifications on offer. These are recognised by some universities who offer Higher Education qualifications to develop your career in the Security Sector.

Working as an academic

As an undergraduate or postgraduate student you are taught, guided and inspired by those who teach you. Academics deliver your lectures, assess your progress, conduct research and write the literature that you use for your own independent learning. This section of the chapter will look at what you may need to do to become an academic yourself; to teach and research within a university setting. We have decided to include this section because there appears to be an increasing interest from students in this as a chosen career path.

What do academics do?

The first thing to remember is that academics do not work 9–5. The job is not predictable and can vary from day to day. Most academics, however, work within a university and have a role that combines teaching, research and administrative duties and responsibilities, and it is most likely that in your first permanent post you would be required to combine and balance these three different aspects. Some academics, however, do have teaching focussed roles (which has a higher teaching commitment than research) and others research-focussed roles (which has a higher research commitment than teaching); this is usually defined by the institution and their goals.

As a guideline the salary scale for a lecturer starts at around £37,000 and this rises incrementally to around £46,000. There is a clearly defined progression route for an academic (although this may vary according to the institution) and your salary will rise according to the position that you hold.

Is an academic career for you?

Becoming an academic is possibly one of the most competitive jobs you could aspire to. It is a competitive profession that requires commitment and dedication. On average it takes a minimum of seven years from starting your journey as an academic to getting your first lectureship.

Reflection point

It is important when considering an academic career that you give some thought to why you are considering this option. In doing this you need to think not only of your motivations but also what you know about the job and whether you have the skills that are required for you to be successful.

Action point

Ask yourself some of these questions:

Can I commit to a minimum of seven years?
Am I likely to get a good first degree?
Do I have a passion for the subject?
Do I enjoy teaching?
Am I organised?

The path to academia?

Every academic career path can be unique with no two academic careers being the same. There isn't a prescribed way to secure a post within a university as the route can differ depending on the institution, the discipline you have studied and your own personal preferences and interests.

Action point

If you are considering an academic career, it is important that you look at the website of the university that you are thinking of applying to. Take time to research the information available.

Most people entering academia in the UK now are required to have a doctoral level qualification, such as a PhD, this may differ where the focus is on more vocational or professional development related courses. Experience in the related field in this situation would then be important. This will depend upon the area/discipline of the work that you are interested in.

For those wanting to pursue an academic career without practical experience the most common route is:

- Undergraduate Degree BA/BSc/LLB;
- Postgraduate Degree MA/MSc/LLM;
- Doctor of Philosophy (PhD) – which can be a taught programme of study or a doctorate in research;
- University Teaching Staff/University Researcher/Lecturer.

As stated earlier becoming an academic is a competitive process and so building up your teaching experience will assist you in your application process. Sessional teaching at a university can be a way for you to do this as can teaching part-time or on an evening course at a further education college. It is also important that you know something about how the higher education sector operates. Knowing the institution is also important. When applying for an academic job you will likely be required to submit an application form where you will need to complete a personal statement, attend for an interview and make a presentation.

Reflection point

Think about what the different stages of the application process require you to demonstrate. Practise the skills that you will need to evidence. Remember you are most likely going to be teaching, so how you conduct your presentation is also about teaching style and engagement.

Working in forensic psychology

Within this section of this chapter the role of a forensic psychologist will be discussed. Forensic psychologists play a vital role in the work of the Criminal Justice System both with offenders and victims, your work as a forensic psychologist can also be crucial to other members of staff that work with both offenders and victims. You may also be required to be involved in research and policy development.

Reflection point

Think about the area of work that you may be interested in. Would working in a prison suit you? Are you more suited to consultancy?

The majority of forensic psychologists work within a prison setting, however it is important that you consider the work in other areas including the National Health Service. What will follow will be a general discussion of the work that as a forensic psychologist you could be involved in, the qualification routes, the recruitment process and what skills you will need to be successful in the role.

Working as a forensic psychologist

As a forensic psychologist you would work with a wide range of people in a variety of settings. You may be based in a number of different settings and so you may be required to travel quite a lot. As a qualified forensic psychologist you can expect to start on a salary of around £25,000. This can and will increase depending upon your level of experience and the setting that you work in. Your salary could increase to around £90,000. (These figures are provided as a guide only.)

> *F* *orensic psychologist*, 'I love my job because no two days are the same. What I wasn't prepared for though was how challenging the work could be and how emotionally tiring it could be. On the other hand it is rewarding, especially when you start to see a change in people's behaviour.'

The British Psychological Society clearly state that the role of a forensic psychologist will require you to be able to apply psychological theory to criminal investigation and to the problems that are linked with criminal behaviour. Your main duties could include:

- supporting Police investigations;
- implementing treatment programmes;
- crime analysis;

- undertaking statistical analysis of offending behaviour;
- carrying out risk assessments;
- writing formal reports;
- training new staff;
- developing treatment programmes;
- advising parole boards;
- working with victims.

Entry requirements

Entry into forensic psychology is not possible without a psychology degree. It is important when you are considering this option that you think about the degree you intend to choose. A British Psychological Society (BPS) accredited degree will lead to you gaining the required qualification that you will need. In addition you will also need to complete a Health and Care Professions Council (HCPC) approved programme of training to be called a forensic psychologist.

Action point

Have a look on the British Psychological Society website for a full list of accredited degree programmes. You will also find information on this site regarding accredited conversion courses.

Once you have an accredited degree you will be required to continue your training and in order to achieve chartered membership status you will need to continue to study for an accredited Master's in Forensic Psychology followed by a BPS Qualification in Forensic Psychology Stage 2. This will last for two years during which you will be supervised in practice. You may continue your studies with a Doctorate in Forensic Psychology.

Previous voluntary or work experience in a related field is usually required before you can start to work as a Forensic Psychologist. This could include work in a prison setting, probation setting or within the voluntary sector. It is important that you start to gain some experience as soon as possible.

Skills and qualities

You will need to demonstrate that you:

- have a keen interest in the cause of criminal behaviour;
- have an understanding of the Criminal Justice sector;
- have a genuine desire to help offenders;
- are resilient;
- are patient;
- are honest;
- have an ability to work well in a team;
- have excellent communication skills;
- are good at problem solving;
- are good at working under pressure;
- can meet deadlines and complete tasks;
- have an interest in research;
- are accurate and logical;
- have good IT skills.

The recruitment process will depend upon the area that you are working in. It will undoubtedly involve the completion of an application form, a competency-based interview and a presentation. A series of eligibility checks will also be carried out.

Action point

Read Chapter 4 of this text as it will assist you in thinking about the different recruitment stages and what you will need to consider.

Chapter summary

This chapter has hopefully encouraged you to think about other career options related to Criminal Justice and the work of the Criminal Justice sector. It is important when considering the careers and options discussed in this chapter that you also refer to the other chapters in this book. Take time to think about the points that we have raised and complete the tasks set. Finally as with the other chapters in this book we have included some top tips for you to remember. Don't forget these. We hope that you have enjoyed learning about other related sectors and that we have broadened the options that you have. Good luck.

Top tips

- Read the other chapters in this book.
- It is important to understand the range of options available in the Criminal Justice sector.
- Understand the work of the third sector and think about the range of options available.
- Look at the CLINKS website.
- Get some work experience, either voluntary or paid.
- Think about why you want the job that you have applied for.
- Can you commit to the length of study that may be required?

- Look at the Do It website for volunteering and work experience opportunities.
- Be aware of your values and motivations.
- Read as widely as possible.
- Think about how you can evidence the skills needed.
- Understand what the recruitment and selection process requires from you; what are the different stages?

Some useful websites

- www.do-it.org.uk (National volunteering website)
- www.victimsupportni.co.uk (The Northern Ireland Victim Support Services)
- www.victimsupportsco.org.uk (Scotland Victim Support)
- www.victimsupport.org.uk (England and Wales)
- www.justice.gov.uk (HM Prison service)
- www.skillsforjustice.com (Sewctor skills council)
- www.bps.org.uk (British Psychological Society)
- www.hpc-uk.org (Health and Care Professions Council)
- www.prospects.ac.uk (Careers and information and advice website for graduates)
- www.clinks.org.uk (Advice and support for third sector organisations)
- www.thirdsector.co.uk (Advice and guidance for third sector organisations)
- www.nhscareers.uk (NHS website with careers information)
- www.sia.homeoffice.gov.uk (Security Industry authority website)
- www.bsia.co.uk (British Security Industry Association website)
- www.security-institute.org (The security institute)
- www.MI5.gov.uk Security Services (MI5)
- www.SIS.gov.uk Secret Intelligence Service (MI6)
- www.addaction.org.uk (Specialist drug and alcohol treatment charity)
- www.turningpoint.co.uk (Services for those with drug, alcohol and mental health problems)
- www.scottishdrugservices.com (Provides details of over 200 agencies in Scotland)
- www.addictionni.com (Provides support and treatment to people affected by drugs)

- www.nta.nhs.uk (drugs interventions programme operational handbook)
- www.communitycare.co.uk (community care website providing social work news and social care jobs)
- www.sssc.uk.com (Scottish social services council choosing a career in social services)
- www.niscc.inf (Northern Ireland social care council)

Recommended reading

There is a wealth of sources that you could refer to in this section. By researching the above websites and the other chapters in this text you will be able to locate the most useful to you.

References

Guardian (Sept 2012) Guardian UK 300 employers. Retrieved from http://targetjobs.co.uk/uk300 (accessed 27 May 2014)

MI5 Employment facts and figures www.MI5.gov.uk

Skills for Security (n.d.) Retrieved from www.skillsforsecurity.org.uk/index.php/securityindustry (accessed 27 May 2014)

chapter 11

Final thoughts

Moving forward and developing a successful career

Chapter objectives

By the end of this chapter you should be able to:

- review and reflect on all the key issues raised in the chapters of this book;
- understand how these issues in Criminal Justice today may impact on you getting a job and developing a career in this sector;
- recognise how best you can deal with these issues and overcome them;
- recognise other careers related to Criminal Justice and how you can make a successful transition into these areas.

You are nearly at the end of your journey through this guide-book. However, the reality is that you may now just be starting your journey into employment in the Criminal Justice sector. This book has been written so you can dip in and out of the chapters to make it as flexible and helpful as possible. In case you have not read all the chapters in depth it may just be useful at this point to summarise the chapters again, as you may have missed something that may be useful for you and you didn't realise was included in the text – you can revisit it now.

> **Action point**
>
> Perhaps now is also the time to go back and review and reflect on the key issues so you feel you have a good understanding of the sector and the issues and challenges you may be facing, and the opportunities you may have. The greater understanding you have at this point, the better prepared you will be.

Chapter 1 *introduces* the book to you and how to use it to its best effect. It has been designed to provide you with up-to-date information as well as advice and guidance. The chapter explains that the text is written to include a number of activities, some to get you to stop and reflect on your knowledge or beliefs and values, as well as some practical advice and activities, all of which are designed to help you consider your own personal career journey and to help you to make well informed decisions and actions to progress this.

Chapter 2 sets the context for the whole of the book by giving you an overview of the *Criminal Justice System*, this is key to many of the issues and concepts discussed throughout the book, so if you have not yet taken the time to get to grips with this information, it is worth going back to this. It discusses the difficulties that exist with defining crime and then goes on to explaining the principle that underpins Criminal Justice within the United Kingdom; adversarial justice and due process. Following this is a brief outline of some common reasons as to why an individual may commit crime, as well as the ways in which crime is recorded and measured. The chapter then goes on to explain the UK's three distinctive Criminal Justice Systems, including some of the agencies involved and how they compare and contrast dependent upon the jurisdiction. The chapter concludes by making reference to the eight different theoretical models of Criminal Justice that seek to justify how the system can operate. It is a very clear summary of the world you may wish to work in, and that you will need a good understanding of in order to decide how and where to develop your career.

Action point

If you have not read Chapter 2, go back and revisit this, it will give you a very good overview and understanding of the sector, even if you already know what agency you would like to work in. Remember the agency operates as an integral part of a bigger system, so take the time to find out how it all fits together.

Chapter 3 gives an explanation of the *academic routes* into a career in Criminal Justice, outlining all the key considerations for students wanting to pursue these routes and how to find out all the information you will need to choose the best course of study for you. It highlights the options of where to study and the types of institutions that offer Criminal Justice and related courses, as well as the variety and range of courses that are available, from Foundation degrees to part-time study. It also covers how to find out more detailed information on these different routes from these institutions and how to compare these courses to help you in your decision-making. Practical information is included in the chapter about making the most of university and college open days to help you research your final choices. In contrast, the chapter also includes apprenticeships or jobs with training as alternative routes into Criminal Justice, and how to find what opportunities are available to you and how to apply.

In Chapter 4 you will find some of the essential elements of *becoming employable*. There is much to think about and the emphasis is clearly on you being, among other things, proactive, organised and confident. Being honest, reflective and willing to get to know yourself is essential, as is understanding as much as possible about the opportunities, organisations and sector you apply to. The chapter demonstrates that 'Getting a job is a job in itself!'

Action point

Make sure you include Chapter 4 as essential reading and don't assume you know this information as you think you want a job or career in a specific agency or organisation within the sector; this chapter is essential for all readers, not just those who are still making up their minds about what routes or careers are possible.

The next chapters of the book look at the key individual agencies operating within the sector. In these you will find current issues and up-to-date information regarding how these operate and the details of their recruitment policies to help you understand what you will need to achieve to be successful in becoming employable within them. Chapter 5 covers the *Probation Systems* in England, Wales, Northern Ireland and Scotland. It explores the different roles available within the service and provides detailed information on the entry criteria, recruitment process and the career progression opportunities available.

Chapter 6 moves into the different roles that are available within the *Police Services* in the UK, focussing on the roles, recruitment and selection processes relating to the role of a Police Officer, a Police Community Support Officer, A Special Constable and that of a Police Leader. Again in the chapter you will find reflection tasks that are aimed to support your understanding and thinking about this work.

Prison Services are covered in Chapter 7 and the different roles that are available inside the UK. Within the chapter there is a discussion about the roles that are available and the particular recruitment and selection processes relating to the role of a Prison Officer and that of a Prison Service Manager.

Chapter 8 considers working within the *Courts and Prosecution Services* within the UK. This chapter explains that there is not one single unified system and as such it is important that you pay attention to the differences between the jurisdictions of England and Wales, Scotland and Northern Ireland. Within the chapter there is separate information about the recruitment processes and practice in the different jurisdictions, although the similarities are noted where they apply. It is important that you consider these differences and the implications of them for the area and role that you wish to apply to and work in.

Chapter 9 looks at working in multi-agency Youth Offending teams, made up of representatives from both the statutory and voluntary organisations. If your preference is working with young people then this may be an area to consider as it has a wide range of opportunities.

The final chapter in this section, Chapter 10, considers briefly some of the *other related agencies and organisations* linked to or associated with Criminal Justice that may be of interest. You may be familiar with some of these already, but it may be worth broadening your scope of vision at this stage of your planning and considering if any of these opportunities may be of interest as well. Remember the Criminal Justice sector is very competitive and it may be that your first choice of career or role is difficult to access initially, even with a good degree, so you may need to consider other options and possible routes of entry in the longer term.

Moving forward

What is hopefully now evident to you, after reading these chapters in more depth, is that being a strong job applicant in the Criminal Justice sector involves many things including acquiring traditional academic skills,

- critical thinking
- analytical research
- intellectual curiosity.

In addition you will require social skills, e.g. emotional intelligence, team working experience, increased confidence and employability skills such as:

- communication
- planning and organising
- project management.

People often refer to 'graduate level' and/or 'graduateness' and attach an assumed credibility, status and skill-set accordingly. Both of these presume that graduates have achieved capabilities and attributes and acquired knowledge in a high, graduate-level way that differentiates them from non-graduates, and have developed the ability to call on and use a whole range of higher level skills and experiences in a transferable way. This makes graduates attractive to a wide range of employers.

These employers often advertise job opportunities to graduates stating that those who possess any academic degree subject will be welcome to apply. In fact, about half of all job vacancies aimed at graduates in any year are available to 'any subject discipline' graduates, in other words graduates could have studied any subject and this will be welcomed. This clearly indicates that these employers value the wealth of general high-level transferable graduate skills and attributes as much as, if not more than, subject-specific knowledge. It is therefore essential for you to reflect on, recognise, identify and articulate these skills and attributes in the best way possible, including in letters of application, CVs, application forms, during selection centres and at interview.

Making a positive connection between the job description for the role, person specification and yourself (the applicant) is essential during the application and interview processes. Interviewers will expect you to articulate your positive attributes, skills and experiences and if you don't then other applicants will, so this is a competitive environment where the winners take all! As someone interested in Criminal Justice you will hopefully have a very wide range of positive things that will set you apart from the competition. The key is to make sure that you reflect in some depth on who you are and what makes your application relevant and different. Some of the activities in the earlier chapters in this book are aimed at helping you do this.

> ## Action point
>
> If you have not completed any of these action points from the previous chapters, consider doing this now. Bring all your information together as you will need to start to document and keep these reflections; you will need to refer back to them at a later stage in your job or university application process.

Once engaged in a job role in your chosen career a number of new questions, opportunities, challenges and choices will present themselves. For example, if you like your job and are challenged and stimulated by it you may want to develop your role internally by seeking new challenges or projects and looking for professional development and promotion. Alternatively you may find that you have achieved most of what you set out to achieve in your role and have entered a career 'cul de sac' with little or no obvious prospect of career development and progression. If this is the case then reconsidering your potential career trajectory, moving on from your current employer and getting another job with a new one might be a sensible next step.

When looking to get on and develop your existing role within your current employer a number of factors are important to consider.

Finding out what is available within your organisation

To find out what is available in your organisation to enable you to grow your career, speak to someone in the human resources or training department, your line manager, more experienced colleagues or a union representative. Looking at an organisation chart that provides details of all the jobs and the departmental structure can be useful. Networking with colleagues, friends and other contacts who know the organisation can also be a source of information and ideas. It is important to keep uppermost in your mind that you must make yourself as strong an applicant as possible in a challenging job market. *This must include you always thinking about yourself in terms of your experiences, success and things you are good at, qualifications, attributes, skills and competencies.*

Developing experience, attributes and skills at work

Opportunities may exist to do this, for example:

- Everyday functions and tasks are almost too obvious to consider but these 'bread and butter' aspects of your role will provide you with essential examples to draw upon when you make claims that you can for example:
  - be organised
  - work independently
  - set objectives and meet them
  - work productively with others
  - be flexible
  - solve problems
  - achieve goals.

Taking an analytical approach to thinking about your role makes sense. In other words break your role up into functions and tasks, think about each one individually and also how, when considered together, all of these things produce results and success.

- *Project work* such as developing a website, organising a survey, conducting research, running a campaign or organising an event could help you gain experience in a different area or develop new skills e.g. project management or take on more responsibility, while enhancing your CV. Again thinking about any projects you have managed or been involved with in an analytical way will help you to explain your contribution in a logical and convincing manner.

final thoughts

- *Secondments or exchanges* might involve working in a partner organisation for a limited period while your existing job role is held open, being covered by other staff. You are usually expected to provide a detailed report of your experience. Secondments aim to benefit your original organisation, while giving you experience and insight into how others operate and allowing you to develop your skills and knowledge. Completing a secondment also shows that you are prepared to be adventurous and accept an element of risk by testing yourself in unfamiliar environments and with new colleagues.
- *Sponsorship* by your employer to undertake further study and professional development can form part of your career or professional development plan. Approaching your employer for sponsorship will mean preparing your case thoroughly and negotiating the funds you want your employer to provide and cover while you are away from work.

Take time to prepare and try these tips to help you make a successful case:

- Think carefully about what you want in terms of your career, clarify your aims and make sure the course you suggest will deliver the outcomes you want.
- Speak to your line manager to test the water and to establish what might be available to you, in other words, is this worth going for?
- Thoroughly research potential study choices and providers, and check what is available through internal training programmes.
- Prepare your 'pitch' thoroughly, thinking about the benefits to your employer as well as to you.
- Explain clearly how you will stay connected to your employer while being sponsored and how you will report back into the organisation all of the things that will bring benefit to the organisation. Perhaps this could include regular updates by email, Skype or visits and short presentations.
- Identify the best value option.

Appraisal schemes and career development programmes benefit you and your employer because they provide an opportunity to reflect on, and discuss, how you are performing against the duties and responsibilities expected of you. This is an opportunity to talk all about you, this is your time and you should optimise this.

These sessions allow the following to take place:

- review your performance to date, including achievements, challenges and areas for development;
- provide helpful, developmental feedback on your performance;
- agree performance targets and objectives for the next period of time, which is normally a year;
- discuss your aspirations and plans and identify how they might connect with the direction and objectives of your employer;
- discuss any potential opportunities for advancement and promotion;
- discuss any agreed gaps in skills and training to enable better performance;
- discuss your career/development plan.

Appraisals tend to be part of the employee career development programmes employers use to ensure that staff are skilled, competent and supported to be able to perform their job role. They should provide an opportunity to consider relevant career/professional development.

A successful appraisal needs to be organised and held in the right setting that encourages discussion and commitment from both you and your appraiser.

Preparing well is essential to making the most of the process. Many employers run short training sessions on how to optimise the appraisal system; alternatively you could ask the human resources or training department for help. In some companies the process may be less organised and formal, but it is important to make the most of these opportunities, so be prepared to ask for time to discuss you and your job role and also prepare as fully as you can.

Note that if you do not have the opportunity to participate in a career development programme or staff appraisal within your organisation, you can still take control and manage your own continuing professional development.

Preparing for appraisals

Take time to prepare for your appraisal or a career development session so that you know what your priorities are and can negotiate effectively for yourself.

While most organisations have their own guidelines for both the appraisee and appraiser, you will most likely be asked to complete an appraisal form before your meeting. Here are some key areas that are covered in most forms; reflecting thoroughly on them will ensure that you make full use of your appraisal.

Your role

Refer back to your job description as a reminder of your role and responsibilities. This assumes that your job description is up to date.

- Which part of your job have you most enjoyed?
- Analyse carefully why you have enjoyed these specific aspects and be prepared to clearly explain and articulate this.
- Which aspects have you found challenging or difficult?
- It is important to be able to explain fully why you have found certain aspects challenging or difficult and be able to suggest ways that you can develop your competence.

Your performance: achievements

Think about your own performance and that of your team over the past year (or since your last appraisal).

- What have your main achievements been?
- Can you rank order these?
- How have you played to your strengths?
- What skills or knowledge have you gained in your role?
- Overall, how have you developed?

Your performance: challenges

- What have been the main challenges for you?
- Where do you feel you have not achieved your potential?
- What are the barriers to reaching your potential?

Your staff development

- What personal development or training have you taken part in?
- How did this affect your role?

Future development

- Which aspects of your role would you like to develop?
- How would this support your work objectives?
- What extra training or work experience do you need to undertake?
- Are there opportunities for sponsorship for relevant study?
- Are there any projects you would like to take part in, or new teams you would like to work with? How would this benefit your unit or organisation?
- What personal development needs do you have in terms of your career path?

Getting a job outside the Criminal Justice sector

Employability is a term that is now often referred to as being important for those seeking work. A widely accepted definition of employability is 'a set of achievements – skills, understandings and personal attributes – that make graduates more likely to gain employment and be successful in their chosen occupations, which benefits themselves, the workforce, the community and the economy' (Pegg *et al.* 2012).

Being able to demonstrate insight into the organisation and sector you are considering as an employment option, how it functions, the environment it operates in and who its customers or clients are, is essential to convince an employer that you are serious about them and you are making a well-informed career move.

This is important because by *developing your organisational awareness* you will be able to make balanced decisions about the type of work you wish to secure. By ensuring that your own values and ethics match that of an organisation, you are taking a significant step towards employment that will be motivating, rewarding and a good fit for you. Also, at both application and interview stages, employers will be looking for evidence that you understand their organisation. Many regard this as absolutely essential. They want to recruit people who care about what the organisation does and who have considered whether they will fit in well, be happy and be able to add value.

To assess this, employers will ask questions such as:

- Why do you want to enter this industry?
- What do you know about our organisation?
- What are our main products/services?
- What do you think the job you would be doing involves?
- What are the challenges facing our industry at this time?
- What changes have there been in our industry recently?
- Who are our competitors? What are the differences between them and us?
- Who are our clients?
- How do you keep up to date with current issues in the sector?

There are *many resources available to you to research an organisation* and the sector in which it operates. One of the first places to start is the organisation's website. It's likely that you will find lots of relevant information here about the history, function, mission, structure, values and culture of the organisation.

Action point

Take a look at the 'working with us' (or similar) web pages for insight into what organisations are looking for in their employees and consider if you are a good match for them. You may find information published for stakeholders, such as investors, particularly useful. Read recent annual reports with details of its performance to analyse key trends for the organisation – very useful to generate a well-informed interview. The business library section at your local city library can be a mine of useful information.

You should also *analyse the job description and person specification* for the role you are interested in. This should help you to identify how to best demonstrate that you meet all of the requirements for the role and produce a suitably tailored application.

Don't be afraid to contact the organisation directly for further information. Employers often value candidates who show a genuine interest by asking for a short meeting or telephone conversation to discuss the role and support their pre-application research.

Social networks can also be a great way to find out accurate, up-to-date information about an organisation and sector.

Action point

You can research a company on LinkedIn and make contact with current employees to help you to develop insight into what it's like to work there and the sector in general. Twitter is also a useful tool for following people who are posting relevant information about their employer or industry. Similarly, a company's pages on Facebook can have valuable information for anyone looking to build a profile of the organisation.

Equally, employers are looking for candidates who can demonstrate that they understand the environment that the organisation operates in. Specific research into the sector or industry can be done by keeping updated with industry publications and professional bodies. You may also want to look at recent market research reports for information on developments, trends, key players and current issues – all good topics for interview questions.

Finally, a good grasp of business/sector issues will ensure that a potential employer views you as being commercially/sector aware. You should be able to analyse and evaluate the impact of issues in areas such as politics, the economy, society and technology on the organisation.

Action point

Follow the organisation for a month or preferably longer in the business/sector/trade press, this should give you a good insight and support your understanding of your chosen organisation and industry.

You have now come to the end of the book and we hope you have found the information we have provided informative and helpful in your career journey into Criminal Justice. If you have decided this is not your chosen route then perhaps we have given you some more ideas and areas to look into to find rewarding and successful careers. Within the text you will have found other links to websites and further reading and resources to help you to continue the next steps of your journey, be it directly into employment or study. This book is not exhaustive in its inform-ation, links or activities, but we hope we have presented the issues for you to consider clearly, raised your awareness of some new issues and challenged your thinking.

There are undoubtedly some highly rewarding but challenging jobs and roles in Criminal Justice in the UK and we hope this book has provided you with insight into not only how to find these but how get into them and build successful careers.

The information here is presented to help you, not just in your first transition into a job but is also intended to demonstrate that developing a successful career or moving career direction is helped by understanding who you are and what you can offer an employer, and as you build your career this personal reflective process will hopefully continue. As you gain more experience from a job or role this adds to your bank of knowledge, skills and attributes that you can then present to a new employer or to your existing employer to secure a new job or promotion. Essentially what is described here is a lifelong process you can use time and time again.

Reference

Pegg, A., Waldcock, J., Hendy-Isaac, S. and Lawton, R. (2012) *Pedagogy for Employability*. York: Higher Education Academy

Index